REED CONCISE GUIDE

FERNS
of Australia

Phlegmariurus squarrosus

David L Jones

First published in 2025 by Reed New Holland Publishers
Sydney

newhollandpublishers.com

A record of this book is held at the National Library of Australia.

ISBN 9781760796341

Managing Director: Fiona Schultz
Publisher and Project Editor: Simon Papps
Designer: Andrew Davies
Production Director: Arlene Gippert
Cover photo: Shutterstock

Printed in China

10 9 8 7 6 5 4 3 2 1

Keep up with Reed New Holland
and New Holland Publishers

ReedNewHolland

@NewHollandPublishers and @ReedNewHolland

Front cover: *Dendroconche scandens*
Back cover: *Angiopteris evecta*

Angiopteris evecta

Diplopterygium longissimum

CONTENTS

INTRODUCTION

The Australian flora (mainland Australia plus offshore island territories) contains 528 species and subspecies of ferns and fern relatives (AKA lycophytes) of which 377 taxa (71 per cent) are endemic (Field 2020). Of the total number of ferns and lycophytes found in the Australian territories, some 471 species in 134 genera occur on the Australian mainland, of which 109 species (23 per cent) are endemic. Despite about one quarter of the mainland fern species being endemic, no fern genus or lycophyte genus is endemic to Australia.

Within mainland Australia, by far the greatest diversity and largest concentration of ferns and lycophytes occurs in Queensland, where some 406 species are found, of which 79 species (19 per cent) are endemic to the state. In Queensland, ferns and lycophytes are especially prominent in the north-east of the state, predominantly in rainforests that extend from the coast to the ranges and tablelands. Some Australian territorial offshore islands also host ferns and lycophytes, particularly Lord Howe Island which is especially fern rich with some 65 species occurring there, of which 23 species (33 per cent) are endemic to the island. Additionally, Norfolk Island contains 45 species (7 endemic) and Christmas Island 30 species (none of which are endemic).

This tiny book contains 187 species of native ferns in 93 genera and 31 families. All these ferns are found on the Australian mainland, a reasonable sample (c.40 per cent) of the species found on this remarkable continent. Common species are well covered but also included are some unusual and rarely seen species which add significance to the publication. Most of the photos are the author's, but a few from other sources help to extend the coverage. Thanks to Ben Wallace for his photo of *Phlegmariurus dalhousieanus* and Chris Goudey for *Asplenium decurrens* and *Azolla pinnata*.

Arrangement of the species: The ferns included in this book are arranged alphabetically by their botanical names within their plant family, and the plant families are arranged alphabetically throughout the text.

Fern names: The text of this book includes at least one common name for each fern species as well as a designated scientific binomial name, which consists of a genus name and species epithet. For example, the common name Fishbone Water Fern is associated with the botanical name of *Lomaria nuda, Lomaria* being the name of the genus and *nuda* being the species name. Botanically, binomial names are more accurately applied than common names, which often arise from general usage or popularity. A species can have several common names but only a single binomial name is accurate within a classification system. Unfortunately, parallel classification systems can be found in some groups of plants, ferns included, and in this example, the applicable alternate binomial name to Fishbone Water Fern is *Blechnum nudum*. The common names used in this book are those that are widely adopted or commonly accepted.

Classification: The family placement of genera used in this book is based on the results of recent molecular-based genetic studies and may cause some confusion to readers since the family placement and generic names used here will often differ from traditional concepts and even those used in the 1998 fern volume of the *Flora of Australia*. For this little book I have followed the 2016 classification proposed by the Pteridophyte Phylogeny Group, which is based on the results of a global systematic approach using modern detailed molecular phylogenetic studies, access to fern collections in herbaria around the world and detailed literature searches. These extensive studies have resulted in changes in the classification of ferns at all levels – class, order, family, subfamily, genus and species – and have impacted significantly on the nomenclature of Australian ferns. Despite these detailed studies some complex groups of ferns, such as members of the families Thelypteridaceae and Polypodiaceae, still require further study and nomenclatural changes in them and some other complex groups are to be expected. I have chosen to follow this modern classification because it is the way of the future and lines up with similar studies in the Orchidaceae, the lilies and many other plant groups, however, it must be acknowledged that not all herbaria, botanists and fern enthusiasts will accept these changes. Consequently, I have included names used in alternative systems of classification (AKA) in the text. In some cases, earlier names are also included (PKA), which will hopefully help to track nomenclatural name changes.

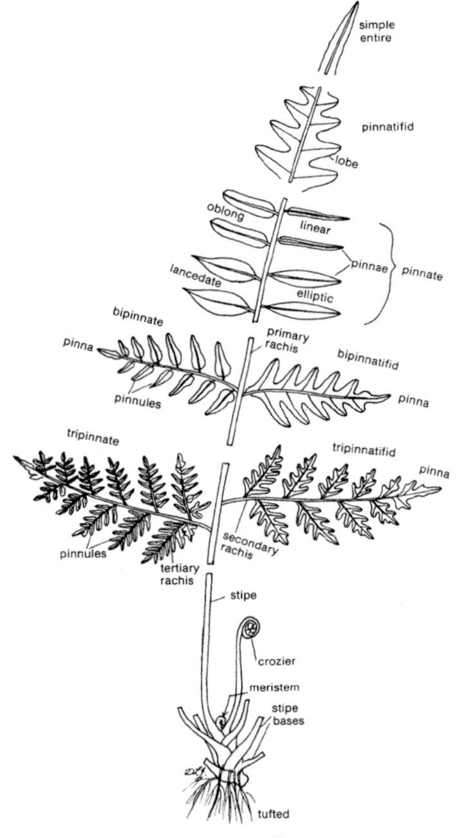
simple
entire
pinnatifid
lobe
oblong
linear
pinnae
pinnate
lancedate
elliptic
bipinnate
primary
rachis
pinna
bipinnatifid
pinnules
pinna
tripinnate
tripinnatifid
pinna
secondary
rachis
pinnules
tertiary
rachis
stipe
crozier
meristem
stipe
bases
tufted

FERN STRUCTURE

Although generally similar in structure to other plants, ferns have also developed some unique specialised features that are important for identification and may require explanation.

Rhizomes: The stems of ferns, generally known as rhizomes, are an important feature for identification. They may be erect with the fronds in a tuft, or creeping with the fronds spaced along the length of the rhizome. Creeping rhizomes are often also distinguished by their length and the distance by which the fronds are spaced apart – using terms such as short-creeping with crowded fronds, medium-creeping (fronds somewhat crowded) or long-creeping with widely spaced fronds. Large upright stems, as in some tree ferns, may also have the appearance of a trunk, the outer surface consisting of a mantle of fibrous roots. A large trunk, as found in tree ferns, is also known as a caudex. Some ferns have climbing rhizomes (termed scandent) that are attached to the supporting host by roots that develop as the rhizome grows.

Scales, hairs and bristles: These structures protect developing shoots, fronds and soft tissue. Scales are flattened papery structures one cell thick and are attached either by a point along the margin of the scale (marginal attachment), or by some point on the underside of their flat surface (peltate attachment). In some scales the cell walls are thickened to form a lattice-like pattern (clathrate scales). Scales vary in colour and shape, and their margins can be smooth, variously toothed, lacerated or hairy. Hairs, which are elongated, thread-like structures of variable abundance, thickness and colour, occur on the organs of some ferns. They can be eglandular (no apical structure or gland) or glandular (with a thickened apical structure). Bristles, a feature of the fern genus *Dipteris*, are rigid hairs with an expanded base more than one cell thick.

Leaves: Fern leaves, usually called fronds, have a basal, petiole-like structure arising from the rhizome which is called a stipe, and an expanded area that is known as the lamina or blade. Stipes can arise directly from the rhizome or be jointed (articulated) on the rhizome or jointed on small outgrowths of the rhizome termed phyllopodia. The lamina (blade) is the prominent expanded part of the frond that is of characteristic shape and division for each species. It is usually green but young emerging fronds can often be pinkish or purplish due to the presence of anthocyanins. Sterile fronds contain no spores or spore-bearing structures, whereas fertile fronds carry spores in spore-bearing structures. Ferns in which the sterile and fertile fronds are of similar in size, shape and division to the fertile fronds are termed monomorphic, whereas ferns with different sized and shaped sterile and fertile fronds are termed dimorphic. Often in dimorphic ferns, the fertile fronds are taller (to aid spore dispersal) and with narrower segments than the sterile fronds. Some climbing ferns have immature basal fronds (bathyphylls) that are quite different in size and shape to the mature fronds. A few ferns with creeping rhizomes have specialised humus-collecting fronds (also sterile) that are of different shape to the other fronds. Developing fronds of many fern species are coiled characteristically like a watch spring – a condition known as circinate vernation. Others have fronds hooked like a shepherd's crook when developing, or are always straight, simply lengthening from the base.

Frond division: Fronds can be simple and unlobed, simple with variously lobed margins or divided into segments. Simple lobed fronds, with the divisions not reaching the midrib (primary rachis), are termed pinnatifid and the segments are called lobes. If the lobes extend right to the primary rachis, the frond is termed pinnate, and the lobes are called pinnae. If the pinnae themselves are lobed, the frond is termed bipinnatifid and if the pinnae themselves are divided to their midrib (secondary rachis), the frond is bipinnate and the segments are called pinnules. Divisions of this type can occur up to 5-pinnate fronds. Some ferns branch by forking (termed dichotomous).

Spores and sporangia: Ferns reproduce by spores, which are tiny, dust-like, single-celled structures that lack an embryo. Spores, which are produced in specialised spore cases known as sporangia, are distributed on air currents when mature. In most ferns, sporangia are clustered in distinct groups called sori (singular sorus) and are carried on the underside of fronds or along the frond margins. Shapes of sporangia vary from round to elongate and in some ferns the sori are scattered over the underside of a frond, sometimes completely covering the lower surface. Sori can be naked and uncovered (termed exindusiate), covered by a thin specialised outgrowth from the frond, known as an indusium, or be covered by reflexed margins of the frond (termed false indusium).

SOME IMPORTANT GROUPS

Tree Ferns: A distinctive group of ferns that are readily recognised by an erect trunk topped by a crown of long, spreading lacy fronds. The fern trunk can be woody or with an outer mantle made up of tough fibrous roots. Developing fronds emerge singly or several at a time in spectacular flushes. Two groups of Australian tree ferns are distinguishable – those in the family Cyatheaceae, which have scales present on the new growth, and members of the family Dicksoniaceae, in which the upper trunk and new growths are covered with coarse hairs.

Filmy ferns: Family Hymenophyllaceae. A unique group of ferns with thin textured to membranous fronds, which in most species are only one cell thick. These ferns are almost always found in high-rainfall habitats, wet gullies or where constant moisture from clouds, fogs or mists is found. The whole surface of their fronds can take up moisture as a liquid or vapour from the atmosphere. They can also lose moisture just as quickly in dry periods. Filmy ferns commonly grow on wet tree bark, tree fern trunks and wet rocks, often forming matted or spreading patches.

Grammitids: A distinctive group of ferns, often small and with simple undivided or lobed/pinnate fronds and creeping rhizomes. They are prominent in tropical regions but also have species in cold temperate regions. Some species form dense matted colonies on rocks, trees and the trunks of tree ferns. These ferns were originally placed in the family Grammitidaceae but molecular studies show a close relationship with the Polypodiaceae where it is now included as subfamily Grammitidoideae.

Gleicheniads: Family Gleicheniaceae. A distinctive group of terrestrial ferns with creeping rhizomes that branch freely, bearing scales or hairs and distinctive upright fronds that branch by apparent forking (termed pseudodichotomous) with apical buds resting while the next pair of branches develop. Mature fronds end up with successive tiered layers and some species can climb into adjacent vegatation. Many species grow in nutrient-poor soils.

Spleenworts: Family Aspleniaceae. A large important group of ferns (c.700 species of *Asplenium*) that is well-developed in Australia (35 species). Includes terrestrial, lithophytic and epiphytic species with an extensive range of growth forms. Scales lattice-like, on rhizomes and fronds, occas. also hairs. Fronds variable in shape and dissection ranging from simple undivided structures to deeply divided lacy fronds, erect or weeping. Sori elongated along veins, protected by elongated indusia. Although mostly from wetter forests, *Asplenium subglandulosum* is a resurrection fern from semi-arid areas. Members of a distinctive group have undivided radiating fronds which form a nest-like structure to trap forest litter into which the fern's roots grow.

Polypodes: Family Polypodiaceae. An extremely variable group of ferns, most of which were originally included in the complex genus *Polypodium*. Mostly epiphytes or lithophytes, they commonly have a creeping rhizome, peltate scales and fronds in two rows, usually jointed to the upper side of the rhizome. Fronds monomorphic or strongly dimorphic, in shape ranging from simple to lobed, pinnate or forking. Sori are usually exindusiate, often rounded and sometimes sunken in the frond surface, occasionally elongate and parallel to the main veins. Species of *Drynaria* and *Platycerium* have specialised sterile fronds that trap humus.

Above: *Pellaea reynoldsii* in drought. Below: *Platycerium veitchii* in dry season.

Resurrection ferns: A group of drought-resistant ferns that grow in arid and semi-arid inland areas where they survive with low and irregular rainfall. Their fronds are generally small and are covered with scales or hairs to reduce water loss. In long dry periods the fronds eventually lose water, the frond margins curl inwards and the whole frond structure becomes desiccated – brown, dry and brittle, appearing as if dead. At this stage the fronds can be crushed to powder. Some fronds in the crown, however, outlast these testing conditions in a state of dormancy, and several days after rain these apparently dead fronds uncurl their segments, refreshen, turn green again and return to normal growth. Many native species of *Cheilanthes* and *Pellaea reynoldsii* are resurrection plants. Several other ferns can also withstand long dry periods with the fronds wilting badly but generally recovering after rain.

Lycophytes: These are not true ferns but rather fern relatives classified in the families Lycopodiaceae, Isoetaceae, Psilotaceae and Selaginellaceae. They do not have a distinctive fern-like appearance, rather they lack fronds and have leaves (often small) scattered along stems or in spirals. These leaves can be all be of similar appearance or of two types – either sterile leaves or fertile leaf-like structures which support sporangia. Sporangia can be borne in leaf axils or on the end of specialised leaves known as sporophylls, which are often crowded into cones (strobili). Some lycophytes produce a single type of spore, others, such as *Isoetes* and *Selaginella*, bear two types of spores (termed heterosporous).

Abbreviations used in the text:

AKA	Also known as
Af	African geopolitical region
As	Asian geopolitical region
c.	circa, approximately
CI	Christmas Island
Dec, Jan, Feb etc	December, January, February, etc
E(e)	East
ID	identification
Indon.	Indonesia
Is.	island(s)
LHI	Lord Howe Is.
N(n)	North
NCal	New Caledonia
NFK	Norfolk Is.
NG	New Guinea
NSW	New South Wales
NT	Northern Territory
Oc	Oceanian geopolitical region
Occas.	Occasional
PKA	Previously known as
Qld	Queensland
Ra.	ranges
S(s)	South
sp.	species singular
spp.	species plural
tlnds.	Tablelands
W(w)	west
WA	Western Australia
SA	South Australia
Vic	Victoria
Tas	Tasmania

Opposite: *Oceanopteris cartilaginea* new frond.

THE FERNS AND LYCOPHYTES

FORKED SPLEENWORT *Asplenium aethiopicum*

Variable fern that often grows in the crevices of granite rocks in WA, as a lithophyte on boulders and in caves in the eastern states, occas. epiphytic on trees.

ID: Rhizomes short-creeping. Stipes blackish at base, green above. Fronds spreading/arching or upright, 2–3-pinnate, to 25 x 12cm, dark green above, paler beneath. Pinnae margins entire, tips deeply incised.

RANGE/HABITAT: Qld (se), NSW, Vic, WA (sw); Af, As, Oc. Sheltered areas in wetter forests.

ATHERTON SPLEENWORT *Asplenium athertonense*

Small fern with graceful arching/pendent dark green fronds that taper from near the base to long drawn-out apex. Occas. plantlets arise near frond tips.

ID: Rhizomes short-creeping. Stipes to 18cm long. Fronds 1–2-pinnate, to 35 x 9cm (including stipe). Lower pinnae lobed, upper pinnae margins toothed.

RANGE/HABITAT: Qld (Windsor Tlnd to Ravenshoe). Endemic. Wet montane/tlnd rainforest. Sheltered mossy rocks, boulders, trees, often near streams.

SIMPLE SPLEENWORT *Asplenium attenuatum*

Fronds of this fern can be simple and undivided or with lobes in the basal third of the frond. Plantlets arise freely near frond tips, often linking plants together.

ID: Rhizomes short-creeping. Stipes dark brown, densely scaly. Fronds arching/sprawling, to 50 x 2.5cm (including short stipe), dark green, dull, parchment-like, papery in dry times.

RANGE/HABITAT: Qld, NSW (Windsor Tlnd to Blue Mtns). Endemic. Humid forests. Earthen banks, rocks, sheltered slopes, base of trees, often near streams.

BIRD'S NEST FERN, CROW'S NEST FERN

Asplenium australasicum

Popular fern that is widely planted as an ornamental for its decorative nest-like crown of radiating litter-trapping fronds. Trapped forest litter decays and nourishes roots.

ID: Rhizomes erect, unbranched. Fronds simple, to 1.8m x 20cm (including stipe), green to yellow-green, leathery. Rachis flat on upper side, strongly keeled beneath. Sori extending more than half frond width.

RANGE/HABITAT: Qld, NSW (McIlwraith Ra. to Tathra); NG, NFK, Oc. Open areas in wetter forests. Trees, rocks, boulders.

CARNARVON SPLEENWORT

Asplenium carnarvonense

Uncommon fern with a restricted distribution. Forms crowded clumps of sprawling dark green shiny fronds on slopes and among rocks. Plantlets near frond tips link plants together.

ID: Rhizomes short-creeping, scaly. Fronds 1-pinnate (occas. 2–pinnate at base), to 50 x 11cm (including stipe), veins prominent; apical frond portion tail-like. Pinnae 12–25 pairs, margins deeply toothed.

RANGE/HABITAT: Qld (Carnarvon Ra.). Endemic. Humid forest and gorges. Sheltered slopes, earthen banks, near streams.

WEDGE SPLEENWORT *Asplenium cuneatum*

Clumping fern with a crown of erect/arching, dark green, shiny, lacy fronds that are widest near base and taper evenly to apex.

ID: Rhizomes short-creeping. Fronds 2–3-pinnate at base, to 55 x 20cm (including stipe), somewhat leathery. Primary pinnae 9–15 pairs, tips blunt or pointed. Pinnule margins incised.

RANGE/HABITAT: Qld (McIlwraith Ra. to Atherton Tlnd); pantropical. Rainforest. Rocks, boulders, trees near streams.

SHORE SPLEENWORT *Asplenium decurrens*

Specialised coastal fern with thick, fleshy, leathery fronds. Commonly grows among rocks and boulders close to sea but occas. occurs in forested areas away from coast. PKA *Asplenium obtusatum*.

ID: Rhizomes short-creeping, stout, occas. woody. Fronds erect/arching, 1-pinnate, to 75 x 13cm (including stipe), pale green, dull. Pinnae 2–18 pairs, margins toothed, tips blunt.

RANGE/HABITAT: NSW (n to Ulladulla), Vic (w), Tas (mainland, Bass Strait Is.), WA (sw); LHI, NZ. Mainly crevices of coastal rocks.

NORTHERN SHORE SPLEENWORT

Asplenium difforme

Tough fern with a restricted coastal distribution. Often grows in salt-spray affected areas close to sea, occas. in coastal scrub. Thick, fleshy, bright green, shiny fronds spread close to the rock surface.

ID: Rhizomes erect. Fronds somewhat dimorphic (sterile fronds less divided than fertile), (1–)2-pinnate at base, to 35 x 15cm (including stipe). Primary pinnae 5–15 pairs.

RANGE/HABITAT: Qld, NSW (Noosa to La Perouse, Kiama); LHI, NFK. Endemic. Coastal headlands, rock outcrops.

NECKLACE FERN *Asplenium flabellifolium*

Familiar fern that forms sprawling colonies among rocks. Spreads by the production of plantlets from thin extended frond tips. Also grows on rotting logs and as an epiphyte on tree ferns and zamiad trunks.

ID: Rhizomes erect. Fronds prostrate/sprawling, 1-pinnate, narrow, to 45 x 4cm (including stipe), bright green. Pinnae 7–30 pairs, fan-shaped or wedge-shaped, margins incised/toothed.

RANGE/HABITAT: Qld (se), NSW, Vic, Tas, SA, WA (sw); NZ. Humid forest, gorges, rock outcrops.

MOTHER SPLEENWORT *Asplenium gracillimum*

Relatively large fern with thin-textured lacy dark green fronds that produce occasional plantlets on the upper surface towards the tips. PKA *Asplenium bulbiferum* subsp. *gracillimum.*

ID: Rhizomes erect. Fronds erect/arching/spreading, 2–3-pinnate, to 100 x 30cm (including stipe). Primary pinnae 15–30 pairs. Ultimate segments narrow (to 4mm wide), margins smooth, tips smooth or lobed.

RANGE/HABITAT: Qld (se), NSW, Vic, SA (se), Tas; NZ. Wetter forests, fern gullies. Trees, tree ferns, rocks, earthen banks.

HARMAN'S NEST FERN *Asplenium harmanii*

Uncommon/rare fern with a restricted distribution. Forms an untidy, litter-collecting rosette of upright fronds. Occas. lateral growths arise from the rootstock of older plants.

ID: Rhizomes erect, branched. Fronds simple, erect/weakly spreading, to 1.3m x 13cm, dark green, leathery, tapered to a long narrow base. Rachis flat on upper side, sharply keeled beneath. Sori extending two-thirds of frond width.

RANGE/HABITAT: Qld (McPherson Ra.), NSW (Border Ra.). Endemic. Rainforest. Basalt boulders, cliffs.

LONG SPLEENWORT *Asplenium longissimum*

Localised fern with strongly weeping/pendent shiny fronds arising in clusters. Frond apices continue growth, producing successively smaller pinnae until a permanent bud is formed.

ID: Rhizomes short-creeping. Fronds pinnate, to 130 x 16cm (including stipe), pale green to bright green. Pinnae spreading widely, narrow (to 1.5mm wide), margins strongly toothed/incised.

RANGE/HABITAT: NT (n); NG, As. Rainforest. Terrestrial, often at base of trees.

NORTHERN BIRD'S NEST FERN *Asplenium nidus*

Widely distributed and common fern of the tropics. In Aust. restricted to lowland areas of ne Qld, growing on trees and rocks, occas. forming extensive colonies on boulder fields.

ID: Rhizomes erect, unbranched. Fronds simple, erect/spreading, to 1.2m x 15cm, green to yellow-green, leathery. Rachis rounded on upper side, flat beneath. Sori extending less than half frond width.

RANGE/HABITAT: Qld (Torres Strait Is. to Bowen); CI, Af, As, Oc. Trees, rocks, boulders in wetter forests; rockpile vegetation.

PAPERY SPLEENWORT *Asplenium paleaceum*

Coarse fern with arching/spreading dark green fronds. Pinnae become paper-textured with incurved margins when dry, refreshing after rain. Plantlets arise near frond tips.

ID: Rhizomes short-creeping, densely scaly. Fronds pinnate, to 55 x 6cm (including stipe), underside densely scaly. Pinnae spreading widely, crowded, margins irregularly and sharply toothed.

RANGE/HABITAT: Qld (McIlwraith Ra. to Maryborough). Endemic. Rainforest, monsoon thickets. Rocks, moist slopes, streambanks, earthen banks.

NARROW-LEAVED NEST FERN

Asplenium simplicifrons

Tropical fern that forms a somewhat untidy litter-collecting rosette of narrow, out-curved dark green fronds with pointed tips.

ID: Rhizomes erect, unbranched. Fronds simple, erect/spreading, to 70 x 3.5cm (including short stipe), narrowed to base, margins smooth/wavy, apex acuminate. Sori extending three-quarters of frond width, not reaching the margin or midrib.

RANGE/HABITAT: Qld (Mt Finnigan to Eungella). Endemic. Rainforest. Coast to ranges/tlnds. Tree trunks (often low down), rocks, rotting logs.

Sori.

BLANKET FERN *Asplenium subglandulosum*

Small drought-tolerant growing in rock crevices, occas. forming densely packed strips of foliage. Fronds shrivel, curl and become brittle in dry times but refreshen after rain. PKA *Pleurosorus subglandulosus.*

ID: Rhizomes very short, thick. Fronds 1–2-pinnate, to 15 x 4.5cm, deep green, covered with soft, brownish spreading hairs. Pinnae 3–10 pairs, fan-shaped, to 20 x 20mm, with round blunt lobes.

RANGE/HABITAT: All states and territories; NZ. Open woodland, gorges, cliffs, rock outcrops.

COMMON SPLEENWORT *Asplenium trichomanes*

Usually found growing on shaded slopes near streams and among rocks (often limestone), this fern is uncommonly encountered in Aust. Widespread overseas.

ID: Rhizomes erect. Fronds pinnate, suberect/sprawling, to 35 x 2cm (including dark stipe), dark green, plantlets absent. Pinnae ovate, round or wedge-shaped, to 10 x 7mm, margins smooth or toothed.

RANGE/HABITAT: NSW, Vic, Tas, SA, WA (sw); NZ, As, Europe, N America. Humid forest, deep shade.

EXCISED SPLEENWORT *Hymenasplenium excisum*

Rare fern recognised by its distinctive pinnae which have a prominent section missing (as if neatly excised) from the lower basal margin. PKA *Asplenium excisum*.

ID: Rhizomes short-creeping, scaly. Fronds pinnate, to 25 x 20cm (including stipe), pale green, thin-textured. Pinnae 10–25 pairs, to 9 x 1.5cm, margins toothed, tips pointed.

RANGE/HABITAT: Qld (Boonjee to Palmerston); As, Oc. Rainforest. Wet banks and beside streams in deep dark gullies; occas. low down on trees.

DAINTREE SPLEENWORT, WILD'S SPLEENWORT *Hymenasplenium wildii*

Rarely seen small fern with graceful arching/pendent bright green fronds that taper from near the base to the apex. PKA *Asplenium wildii.*

ID: Rhizomes short-creeping, scaly. Fronds pinnate, to 20 x 4cm (including thin, dark stipe), thin-textured. Pinnae 5–8 pairs, to 25 x 11mm, a small section of the lower basal margin appearing as if neatly excised.

RANGE/HABITAT: Qld (Daintree Region). Endemic. Lowland rainforest. Rocks and wet banks beside small streams.

AUSTRAL LADY FERN *Diplazium australe*

Delicate fern with a short, erect, woody trunk and broadly triangular, arching/spreading, dark green, fleshy, lacy fronds that are surprisingly brittle and easily damaged.

ID: Rhizomes to 8cm long. Fronds 3-pinnate, to 2m x 90cm (including stipe), thin textured. Pinnules to 25 x 10mm, margins bluntly toothed or shallowly lobed, apex blunt.

RANGE/HABITAT: Qld (n to Eungella), NSW, Vic (s), Tas; NFK, NZ. Shady gullies and flats in wetter forests.

TICK FERN *Diplazium proliferum*

Robust fern with graceful arching fronds. Plantlets arise in the upper pinnae axils and take root on contact with the ground. Often in localised patches. PKA *Callipteris prolifera*.

ID: Rhizomes tufted, woody, black. Fronds pinnate, 1–2m long, 40–60cm wide, pale green to bright green. Pinnae to 30 x 5.5cm, margins entire or weakly lobed.

RANGE/HABITAT: Qld (Daintree to Cardwell); Af, As, Oc. Sheltered slopes and wet gullies in lowland rainforest.

Sori.

Plantlets.

QUEENSLAND LADY FERN

Diplazium queenslandicum

Graceful fern with an erect trunk and widely spreading, broadly triangular, dark green fronds that are lustrous when wet. The photo shows a relatively small plant displaying its lacy fronds.

ID: Rhizomes to 1m long, scaly. Fronds 3-pinnate, to 2.2m x 90cm (including stipe), membranous, shiny when wet. Pinnules to 12 x 6mm, margins shallowly lobed, apex blunt.

RANGE/HABITAT: Qld (Windsor Tlnd to Evelyn Tlnd, Eungella). Endemic. Sheltered slopes, gullies, streambanks in upland rainforest.

Crozier.

STRAP WATER FERN *Austroblechnum patersonii*

Common fern with either simple undivided, thin, strap-like fronds (subsp. *patersonii*, photo above) or dissected fleshy fronds with 2–8 spreading lobes (subsp. *queenslandicum*). Young fronds pink/bronze. PKA *Blechnum patersonii*.

ID: Rhizomes erect, tufted. Fronds to 90cm long, dark green, margins often toothed. Sterile fronds/lobes 10–30mm wide, fertile fronds/lobes 3–10mm wide.

RANGE/HABITAT: Qld (n to s), NSW, ACT, Vic, Tas (n); LHI. Endemic. Streambanks, rotting logs and rocks in dense wet forests.

Subsp. *queenslandicum*.

ALPINE WATER FERN

Austroblechnum penna-marina subsp. *alpina*

Small fern in dense, spreading patches, sometimes low and mat-like. Sterile fronds shorter, wider and with broader pinnae than fertile fronds. PKA *Blechnum penna-marina*.

ID: Rhizomes long-creeping. Sterile fronds to 40cm x 25mm, pinnate, dark green, with pinnae 4–6mm wide. Fertile pinnae 1–2.5mm wide.

RANGE/HABITAT: NSW, ACT, Vic, Tas; NZ, Macquarie Is., Oc. Montane to alpine swamps, sphagnum bogs, herbfields, forests. Extends to lowland areas in Tas.

SHARP WATER FERN *Diploblechnum acuminatum*

Uncommon fern which grows on steep slopes near streams in dense highland rainforest. Sterile fronds have much wider pinnae than fertile fronds and bear occasional axillary bulbils that can form plantlets. PKA *Pteridoblechnum acuminatum.*

ID: Rhizomes short-creeping. Fronds dimorphic. Sterile fronds to 70 x 30cm, pinnate, bright green, shiny, with prominent veins. Sterile pinnae 15–35mm wide, sharply pointed. Fertile pinnae 2–3mm wide.

RANGE/HABITAT: Qld (Mt Spurgeon, Mt Carbine, Mt Lewis). Endemic.

Young plant.

PRICKLY RASP FERN *Doodia aspera*

Widespread common fern that spreads by rhizomes to form large colonies. Fronds harsh/prickly to the touch. Developing fronds in shades of bright pink-red. AKA *Blechnum neohollandicum.*

ID: Rhizomes erect, densely scaly. Fronds not dimorphic, to 50 x 10cm, pinnatifid, dark green, stiff to leathery.

RANGE/HABITAT: Qld (n to Mossman), NSW, Vic (e); LHI, NZ. Sheltered areas of open forest, wetter forests including rainforest.

New fronds.

SMALL RASP FERN *Doodia caudata*

Frequently encountered fern usually recognised by its narrow, dimorphic fronds. Fertile fronds longer than sterile and with narrower, widely spaced pinnae. Developing fronds pale or pinkish. AKA *Blechnum rupestre, B. spinulosum.*

ID: Rhizomes erect or creeping. Fronds to 40 x 3cm, pinnate. Sterile fronds often prostrate. Fertile fronds upright.

RANGE/HABITAT: Qld (n to Mareeba), NSW, Vic (s), Tas (n, rare), SA (e); LHI. Endemic. Sheltered areas of open forest, wetter forests, stream banks.

Fertile fronds.

FISHBONE WATER FERN *Lomaria nuda*

Common fern often seen in extensive spreading colonies. Old plants can form trunks. Sterile fronds longer and with wider pinnae than fertile fronds (which arise in central groups). PKA *Blechnum nudum.*

ID: Rhizomes erect. Stipes black. Sterile fronds to 1m x 20cm, pinnate, bright green, with pinnae 5–10mm wide. Fertile pinnae 2–4mm wide.

RANGE/HABITAT: Qld (n to s), NSW, ACT, Vic, Tas, SA. Endemic. Coastal to montane humid forests.

Fertile fronds.

GRISTLE FERN *Oceaniopteris cartilaginea*

Tough fern typically found growing on exposed slopes and gullies in bright light but also occurring in shady forests, including rainforest. Forms colonies by stolons. Fronds are usually pale yellow-green, greener when in shade. New fronds bronze/pink. Frequently hybridises with *Doodia aspera*. PKA *Blechnum cartilagineum*.

ID: Rhizomes erect or creeping. Fronds not dimorphic, to 2m x 25cm, leathery. Pinnae 5–15mm wide.

RANGE/HABITAT: Qld (n to Iron Ra.), NSW, ACT, Vic. Endemic. Coastal to montane forests in well-drained soil.

In rainforest.

ROSY WATER FERN *Parablechnum articulatum*

Renowned for its bright rosy-pink new fronds, this fern grows on rocks and boulders in or close to small streams. Sterile fronds have much wider pinnae than fertile fronds. PKA *Blechnum articulatum*.

ID: Rhizomes erect, occas. a short trunk. Fronds dimorphic. Sterile fronds to 1.5m x 50cm, pinnate, dark green, shiny, with spreading pinnae tapered to each end, 10–25mm wide. Fertile pinnae 2–4mm wide.

RANGE/HABITAT: Qld (Cooktown to Cardwell). Endemic. Montane rainforest.

Colourful new frond.

HARD WATER FERN *Parablechnum wattsii*

Common, vigorous fern that often dominates the ground flora, growing in extensive, thick, entangling colonies. New fronds bronze/pink. PKA *Blechnum wattsii*.

ID: Rhizome creeping, branching freely. Fronds dimorphic. Sterile fronds to 1.4m x 25cm, pinnate, dark green, leathery, with spreading pinnae, 10–34mm wide, margins toothed. Fertile pinnae 1.5–2.5mm wide.

RANGE/HABITAT: Qld (n to Eungella), NSW, ACT, Vic, Tas, SA. Endemic. Wetter forests including rainforest.

Colourful new frond.

WOOROONOORAN *Parablechnum wurunuran*

Handsome fern that is commonest high in the mountains (to 1,800m on Mt Bellenden Ker) but can also be seen at lower elevations. New fronds bright pink/red. PKA *Blechnum wurunuran*.

ID: Rhizomes erect to shortly creeping. Fronds dimorphic. Sterile fronds to 1.3m x 40cm, pinnate, dark green, shiny, with spreading pinnae 10–23mm wide, margins finely toothed. Fertile pinnae 3–4mm wide.

RANGE/HABITAT: Qld (Mt Finnigan to Paluma). Endemic. Rainforest from lowlands to mountain tops.

New frond.

CLIMBING SWAMP FERN *Stenochlaena palustris*

Vigorous scrambling terrestrial or high-climbing fern with dark green, shiny dimorphic fronds. Fertile fronds have very narrow pinnae, the underside covered with brown sporangia.

ID: Rhizomes scandent, branching freely. Fronds pinnate, to 150 x 30cm. Sterile pinnae to 20 x 5cm, leathery. Fertile pinnae to 20cm long, 2–3mm wide.

RANGE/HABITAT: WA (n), NT (n), Qld (Torres Strait Is. to Cardwell); As, Oc. Lowland rainforest, swamp forest. Forest margins, embankments, stream banks.

SWAMP WATER FERN *Telmatoblechnum indicum*

Sun-loving fern with stiffly upright fronds. Forms dense spreading colonies in wet habitats. Sterile and fertile fronds are similar in size and shape. Young fronds reddish/bronze. PKA *Blechnum indicum.*

ID: Rhizomes long-creeping to erect. Fronds to 1.5m x 25cm, pinnate, green, shiny, with numerous spreading pinnae to 15cm x 15mm, margins finely toothed.

RANGE/HABITAT: Qld (n to s), NSW, WA (n), NT (n); As, Oc. Coastal swamps, floodplains, paperbark woodland.

New fronds.

ROUGH TREE FERN *Alsophila australis*

Common, hardy tree fern that often colonises moist sites on hillsides and disturbed areas, including roadsides and embankments. PKA *Cyathea australis*.

SIZE/ID: Trunk to 15m x 40cm, basal part with fibrous roots, upper part covered with persistent rough/prickly stipe bases. Fronds to 4m long (including stipe), bipinnate, emerging upright then spreading or drooping, bright green. Pinnae c.50cm long.

RANGE/HABITAT: Qld (se), NSW, ACT, Vic, Tas. Endemic. Coast to ranges in wetter forests and fern gullies.

Crozier.

WIG TREE FERN *Alsophila baileyana*

Distinctive tree fern readily identified by the unusual cluster of deeply dissected (skeletonized) leaflets on the top of the slender trunk. Occas. forms suckers. PKA *Cyathea baileyana*.

SIZE/ID: Trunk to 5m x 10cm, lower part woody with stipe scars, upper part with red-brown stipe bases. Fronds to 2.2m long, bipinnate, widely spreading, bright green, glossy. Pinnae to 60cm long

RANGE/HABITAT: Qld (Windsor Tlnd to Evelyn Tlnd). Endemic. Deep wet gullies in rainforest above 850m alt.

Wig on trunk apex.

REBECCA'S TREE FERN *Alsophila rebeccae*

A graceful tree fern recognised by its slender trunk and widely spreading crown of glossy green fronds. Colonises roadsides and other disturbed sites in rainforest, often in quite sunny locations. Produces suckers from subterranean stolons. PKA *Cyathea rebeccae*.

SIZE/ID: Trunk to 6m x 10cm, upper part with appressed stipe bases. Fronds to 2m long, bipinnate. Pinnae to 60cm long

RANGE/HABITAT: Qld (Iron Ra. to Byfield). Endemic. Wetter forests, including rainforest.

LACY TREE FERN *Cyathea robertsiana*

A very slender tree fern with a narrow woody trunk, the apex green and fleshy, and a graceful crown of spreading, dull, pale green fronds. Colonises sunny roadsides in highland/montane rainforest. PKA *Alsophila robertsiana*.

SIZE/ID: Trunk to 7m x 4–8cm, occas. with a buttress of wiry roots. Fronds to 2.5m long, bipinnate. Pinnae to 50cm long, underside softly hairy.

RANGE/HABITAT: Qld (Cooktown to Eungella). Endemic.

Fleshy trunk apex.

PRICKLY TREE FERN *Sphaeropteris australis*

Slender tree fern with very sharp blackish spines on the stipe bases. These brittle spines can inflict a painful wound on careless botanists. PKA *Cyathea leichhardtiana*.

SIZE/ID: Trunk to 7m x 15cm, covered by stipe bases in younger plants, coin-spotted in older plants. Fronds to 3m long, bipinnate, dark green, shiny, paler beneath. Pinnae to 70cm long.

RANGE/HABITAT: Qld (s from Rockhampton, disjunct at Eungella, Mt Elliot and Mt Bellenden Ker), NSW, Vic (e). Endemic. Rainforest.

Trunk apex.

STRAW TREE FERN, SCALY TREE FERN

Sphaeropteris cooperi

Fast growing tree fern with the croziers, trunk apex and stipe bases covered with silky, pale brown scales. Prominent, oval coin spots on the trunk left by fallen fronds are also a feature. Naturalises readily. PKA *Cyathea cooperi*.

SIZE/ID: Trunk to 15m x 15cm, often with a basal root buttress. Fronds to 4m long, bipinnate, bright green. Pinnae to 70cm long.

RANGE/HABITAT: Qld, NSW (Cooktown to Durras Mtn). Endemic. Open/disturbed areas in wetter forests.

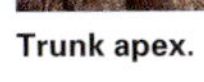

Trunk apex.

Crozier.

COMB HARE'S-FOOT *Davallia pectinata*

Decorative fern restricted to the tropics. Grows in exposed situations on trees and rocks, with the slender scaly rhizomes spreading over the surface and through other epiphytes. Also, on earthen banks.

SIZE/ID: Rhizomes long-creeping, thin, brown scaly when young, white with age. Fronds pinnatifid, narrowly triangular, to 20 x 8cm, leathery, dark green.

RANGE/HABITAT: Qld (Torres Strait Is., Iron Ra., McIlwraith Ra.); As, Oc. Rainforest.

HARE'S-FOOT FERN *Davallia pyxidata*

Common epiphytic fern often seen in the clumps of large epiphytes with its thick chalky, scaleless rhizomes projecting into the air. Fronds are shed in dry times. AKA *Davallia solida* var. *pyxidata*.

SIZE/ID: Rhizomes long-creeping, densely scaly when young. Fronds 2–3-pinnate, dimorphic, triangular, to 75 x 30cm, leathery, bright green. Fertile fronds with narrower segments than sterile fronds.

RANGE/HABITAT: Endemic. Qld (n to Cooktown), NSW, Vic (w); Oc. Coast/ranges in wetter forests.

DWARF HARE'S-FOOT *Davallia repens*

Ornamental small fern with slender rhizomes that spread over tree trunks, rocks and soil. Grows in exposed situations on forest margins. Fronds curl in dry times, refreshening after rain.

SIZE/ID: Rhizomes long-creeping, thin, scaly when young, white with age. Fronds pinnatifid, broadly triangular, to 20 x 12cm, leathery, dark green. Basal pinnae larger and more deeply lobed than others.

RANGE/HABITAT: Qld (Iron Ra. to Eungella); As, Oc. Rainforest.

SCALY HARE'S-FOOT *Davallia solida*

Clumping fern on trees rocks and the ground, the scaly rhizomes adhering closely to the surface and not projecting into the air. Fronds can be shed completely in dry periods.

SIZE/ID: Rhizomes long-creeping, thick, fleshy, scales persistent. Fronds 2–3-pinnate, dimorphic, triangular, to 90 x 40cm, papery, bright green. Fertile fronds with narrower segments than sterile fronds.

RANGE/HABITAT: Qld (Temple Bay to Innisfail); As, Oc. Rainforest and rainforest margins.

LACY GROUND FERN *Dennstaedtia davallioides*

Spreading terrestrial fern with delicate, finely divided, lacy fronds that arise from long-creeping, freely branching rhizomes. Often forms spreading colonies in cool shaded sites.

SIZE/ID: Rhizomes woody. Stipes densely hairy. Fronds broadly triangular, to 1.5m x 70cm, 3–4-pinnate, bright green. Sori in a cup-shaped indusium.

RANGE/HABITAT: NT, Qld (n to Townsville), NSW, ACT, Vic. Endemic. Coast/ranges in wetter forests, streambanks, alluvial flats.

BATS' WING FERN, OAK FERN *Histiopteris incisa*

Distinctive fern recognised by pale green/glaucous fronds with opposed pairs of pinnae and pinnules. The lowest pair of pinnae on each secondary rachis impart the appearance of bat wings or butterfly wings.

SIZE/ID: Rhizomes creeping, much branched, red-scaly. Fronds to 2 x 1m, 3–4-pinnate.

RANGE/HABITAT: NT, Qld (n to Atherton Tlnd), NSW, ACT, Vic, Tas, SA (se); LHI, NFK, Af, As, Oc. Coast/ranges in forest, streambanks, swamps, springs, drains.

HARSH GROUND FERN *Hypolepis muelleri*

Colony-forming fern with dark green fronds similar in appearance to bracken but softer to the touch. Fronds have numerous colourless hairs on the underside veins. Often colonises poorly drained sites.

SIZE/ID: Rhizomes long-creeping, much branched, hairy. Stipes yellow-brown, hairy. Fronds broadly triangular, to 1.8m x 70cm (including stipe), 3-pinnate, somewhat shiny.

RANGE/HABITAT: Qld (n to Atherton Tlnd), NSW, ACT, Vic, Tas (ne). Endemic. Open forest, streambanks, swamps.

BRACKEN FERN *Pteridium esculentum*

An indicator of good drainage, this tenacious fern grows in spreading colonies in a wide range of habitats over much of Aust. Responds strongly to bush fires. Abundant in frequently burnt forests.

SIZE/ID: Rhizomes long-creeping, blackish, hairy. Fronds to 2.5(–3) x 1m, 3–4-pinnate, dark green, tough, leathery. Sori protected by reflexed frond margins.

RANGE/HABITAT: All states, uncommon/rare in tropics; LHI, NFK, As. Coast to alps in forests, heath, pastures.

COMMON GROUND FERN, RAINBOW FERN

Calochlaena dubia

Forests, roadsides and streambanks are clothed by the soft fronds of this very common fern which grows in massed colonies. Usually pale green in shade, the fronds are bleached yellow-green in sun. PKA *Culcita dubia*.

SIZE/ID: Rhizomes creeping, much branched, hairy. Stipes hairy, as long as the blade. Fronds to 1.5m x 80cm, 3–4-pinnate, sparsely hairy, dull, leathery.

RANGE/HABITAT: Qld (se), NSW, ACT, Vic, Tas; Oc. Coast/ranges, open forest, disturbed sites.

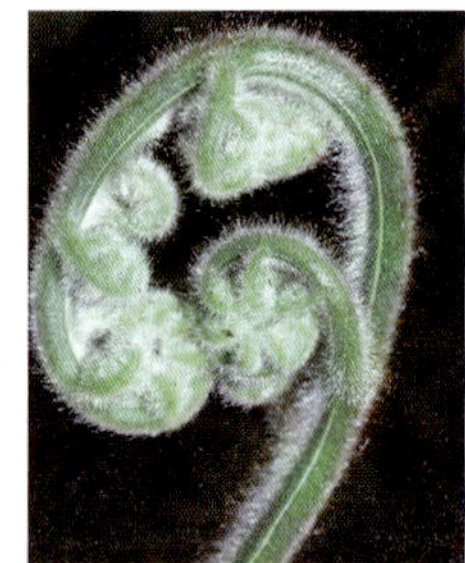

Crozier.

SOFT TREE FERN *Dicksonia antarctica*

Widely distributed tree fern that forms colonies in wetter forests and gullies, sometimes forming extensive pure stands.

SIZE/ID: Trunk to 15m x 40cm, soft, fibrous, covered in a weave of brown aerial roots. Stipes densely hairy, persistent near crown. Fronds to 4m x 70cm, in a large spreading crown, arising in spectacular flushes, 3-pinnate, dark green, glossy, leathery.

RANGE/HABITAT: Qld (se), NSW, ACT, Vic, Tas. Endemic. Coast/ranges in wetter forests, fern gullies.

BRISTLY TREE FERN *Dicksonia herbertii*

Distinctive tree fern confined to the higher peaks and tlnds of ne Qld. Easily recognised by the erect/arching fronds, narrow reddish trunk and numerous reddish or purple-brown, stiff, bristly irritant hairs on the stipes and developing fronds. Mostly found growing singly.

SIZE/ID: Trunk to 4m x 15cm. Fronds to 3m x 70cm, 3-pinnate, pale green, dull, leathery.

RANGE/HABITAT: Qld (Mt Lewis to Eungella). Endemic. Wet montane tropical rainforest.

BUTTERFLY FERN *Dipteris conjugata*

Unmistakable fern which has large, impressive fronds divided into 2 fan-shaped halves, each half then further divided and deeply lobed. Fronds can end up being almost circular with drooping tips.

ID: Rhizomes long-creeping, to 15mm diam., wiry, with stiff red-brown bristles. Stipes to 2.5m long. Fronds crowded, to 1.2m across, pale green to dark green, glaucous beneath.

RANGE/HABITAT: Qld (Atherton Tlnd, Evelyn Tlnd); As, Oc. Rainforest margins, embankments, disturbed sites.

RIPPLED FERN *Bolbitis quoyana*

Handsome colony-forming fern reproducing by plantlets produced on the frond tips. Fronds pinnate, strongly dimorphic. Sterile fronds dark bluish-green, shiny and with rippled margins.

ID: Rhizomes short-creeping. Stipes to 50cm long, scaly. Sterile fronds to 1.2m x 35cm. Pinnae to 20 x 4cm, margins bluntly lobed. Fertile fronds erect on a long stipe and with short, narrow, pale pinnae.

RANGE/HABITAT: Qld (Iron Ra. to Johnstone R.); As, Oc. Wet areas in lowland rainforest.

LARGE TONGUE FERN *Elaphoglossum callifolium*

Distinctive clumping fern with simple, undivided, dark green leathery fronds, shiny on the upper surface, paler and dull beneath. Black crystal-like sporangia cover the undersurface of fertile fronds. Large boulders and tree trunks in upland rainforest.

ID: Rhizomes short-creeping. Fronds to 60 x 6cm. Fertile fronds shorter, narrower and on longer stipe than sterile fronds.

RANGE/HABITAT: Qld (Windsor Tlnd to Eungella.); As, Oc. Rainforest.

SMALL TONGUE FERN

Elaphoglossum queenslandicum

Similar to the previous species but with smaller ellipse-shaped fronds that narrow to each end. Distinctive fertile fronds, smaller than sterile fronds, are carried on longer stipes. The underside is covered with sugar-like blue-black sporangia.

ID: Rhizomes short-creeping. Fronds to 30 x 3cm, dark green and shiny above, paler beneath.

RANGE/HABITAT: Qld (Mt Finnigan to Eungella). Endemic. Rocks, boulders and trees near streams in highland rainforest.

BRISTLY SHIELD FERN *Lastreopsis hispida*

Uncommon fern with finely divided but harsh-textured fronds. Occas. epiphytic on tree ferns. Distributed sporadically and often in localised small patches.

ID: Rhizomes long-creeping. Stipes to 45cm long, covered with stiff red-brown bristles. Fronds crowded, 3–4-pinnate, to 45 x 30cm, triangular, lacy, dark green, roughened, segments with narrow sharp teeth.

RANGE/HABITAT: NSW (Mt Wilson), Vic, Tas; NZ. Wetter forests. Shady, wet, humus-rich soil and rotting logs on sheltered slopes and gullies.

RATTLESNAKE FERN *Lastreopsis poecilophlebia*

Common clumping fern with coarse, dark green pinnate fronds. Pairs of large spreading strongly veined leaflets have toothed margins and extended drawn-out tips. PKA *Coveniella poecilophlebia*.

ID: Rhizomes long-creeping. Stipes densely hairy. Fronds to 95 x 35cm (including stipe). Leaflets 1–6 pairs, Apical leaflet similar.

RANGE/HABITAT: Qld (Iron Ra. to Seaforth). Endemic. Wetter forests. Wet, humus-rich soil and rotting logs on sheltered slopes and gullies.

BROAD SHIELD FERN *Lastreopsis tenera*

Coarse fern with strongly creeping rhizomes and broad, pale green, softly hairy lacy fronds. Forms spreading colonies that dominate the ground flora in some tropical forests.

ID: Rhizomes creeping. Stipes to 75cm long, roughened. Fronds 4-pinnate, to 70 x 60cm, broadly pentagonal, soft white hairs on both sides.

RANGE/HABITAT: Qld (McIlwraith Ra. to Cania Gorge); As, Oc. Coast/ranges and tlnds in sheltered areas of humid open forest, wetter forests, rainforest margins.

LACE FERN *Lastreopsis tripinnata*

Delicate clumping fern with hairy stipes and finely divided lacy fronds. Highly localised and rarely seen. PKA *Oenotrichia tripinnata.*

ID: Rhizomes short-creeping, densely scaly. Stipes to 22cm long, yellow-brown, densely clothed with fawn/white hairs. Fronds upright/spreading in a compact crown, 3–4-pinnate, to 25 x 16cm, dark green, sparsely hairy on both sides.

RANGE/HABITAT: Qld (Windsor Tlnd to Atherton Tlnd). Endemic. Streambanks and rocks in or close to small streams in dense highland rainforest.

Sori.

COARSE SHIELD FERN *Lastreopsis walleri*

Large fern with thick rhizome and coarse, dull coloured, green to grey-green fronds. Often grows in bright light. Occas. beside forestry roads with the fronds spilling down the banks.

ID: Rhizomes robust, short-creeping, very thick, densely scaly. Stipes to 90cm long, roughened, densely scaly and hairy. Fronds to 100 x 90cm, 3-pinnate, pentagonal, covered with short white hairs.

RANGE/HABITAT: Qld (Windsor Tlnd to Evelyn Tlnd). Endemic. Sheltered slopes in open forest and montane rainforest.

TRIM SHIELD FERN *Parapolystichum decompositum*

Distinctive fern with broadly triangular, green to grey-green, hairy, somewhat stiff-textured fronds. Can form crowded patches that dominate the ground flora of some forests. PKA *Lastreopsis decomposita*.

ID: Rhizomes short-creeping, densely scaly. Stipes to 50cm long, scaly and hairy, roughened. Fronds crowded, 3–4-pinnate, to 50 x 50cm.

RANGE/HABITAT: Qld (disjunct on Windsor Tlnd, mainly se), NSW, Vic (e). Endemic. Flats and gullies in wetter forests, especially rainforest.

Sori.

SMOOTH SHIELD FERN *Parapolystichum smithianum*

Localised and generally uncommon, this handsome fern, with its broadly triangular, dark green, somewhat shiny fronds, is tolerant of dark gloomy situations. PKA *Lastreopsis smithiana*.

ID: Rhizomes tufted, erect, with persistent old stipes. Stipes to 55cm long, blackish, glossy. Fronds crowded, 3–4-pinnate, to 50 x 50cm, broadly triangular, thin-textured, dark green, glossy, underside paler.

RANGE/HABITAT: Qld, NSW (Eungella to Lismore). Endemic. Ranges/tlnds in rainforest, often close to streams.

Sori.

DISSECTED SHIELD FERN

Parapolystichum tinarooense

Highly decorative localised fern with crowded, elegantly dissected, lacy, pale green to dark green, shiny fronds. Grows in loose groups in dark humid situations. PKA *Lastreopsis tinarooensis.*

ID: Rhizomes tufted, erect. Stipes to 22cm long, thin, pale green. Fronds 3–4-pinnate, to 25 x 25cm, ±triangular, dull and paler beneath.

RANGE/HABITAT: Qld (Carbine Tlnd to Mt Bartle Frere). Endemic. On rocks in or close to small streams in dense highland rainforest.

MT WINDSOR SHIELD FERN

Parapolystichum windsorense

Handsome fern with a restricted distribution, but occas. locally common. Has decorative arching/spreading, pentagonal, shiny, bright green to dark green fronds. Grows singly or in loose groups in gravelly granitic soil. PKA *Lastreopsis windsorensis*.

ID: Rhizomes short-creeping, apex scaly. Stipes to 75cm long, pale, base scaly. Fronds crowded, 3–4-pinnate, to 70 x 50cm, thin textured, dull and paler beneath.

RANGE/HABITAT: Qld (Windsor Tlnd). Endemic. Sheltered slopes in rainforest.

ROCK SHIELD FERN *Polystichum fallax*

This fern is notable for its densely scaly rhizomes and stipe bases, and shiny dark green leathery fronds that are harsh to the touch. Prefers drier inland western slopes at moderate altitudes. Usually grows among rocks.

ID: Rhizomes erect. Fronds crowded, 2–3-pinnate, to 75 x 35cm (including stipe), no proliferous buds.

RANGE/HABITAT: Qld, NSW (McPherson Ra. to Merriwa). Endemic. Open forest. Sheltered slopes and gullies.

MOTHER SHIELD FERN *Polystichum proliferum*

Reaching its best development in cool wet montane areas, this common fern often grows in extensive colonies. Plantlets take root as the fronds age and become separate plants. Flushes of new unfurling fronds are a decorative feature in spring.

ID: Rhizomes erect, trunk-like, to 10cm tall. Fronds crowded, 2–3-pinnate, to 90 x 40cm (including stipe), dark green, leathery.

RANGE/HABITAT: NSW (n to Tenterfield), ACT, Vic (s), Tas. Endemic. Wetter forests.

New fronds.

LEATHERY SHIELD FERN *Rumohra adiantiformis*

Handsome clumping fern with broadly triangular, leathery, glossy, green to yellow-green fronds. Commonly epiphytic on the fibrous trunks of tree ferns; also on rotting logs, rocks and occas. in the ground.

ID: Rhizomes long-creeping, densely scaly. Stipes often as long as the blade. Fronds 2–4-pinnate, to 90 x 40cm (including stipe).

RANGE/HABITAT: Qld (n to Cairns), NSW, Vic (s), Tas (nw); NZ, Af, As, Oc. Wetter forests including rainforest, fern gullies.

BRIGHT'S CLIMBING FERN *Teratophyllum brightiae*

High-climbing fern which begins life as a young plant creeping over the ground. Juvenile fronds (termed bathyphylls) are easily mistaken for a separate species.

ID: Rhizomes scandent, slender, wiry, naked, apex scaly. Fronds 1-pinnate, dark green, shiny. Juvenile fronds to 25 x 7cm. Mature sterile fronds to 75 x 25cm, semi-weeping. Pinnae to 12 x 1.5cm. Fertile fronds with narrow pinnae 1–2mm wide.

RANGE/HABITAT: Qld (well separated n and s populations). Endemic. Rainforest.

Juvenile fronds.

SCRAMBLING FERN

Dicranopteris linearis var. *linearis*

Common scrambling fern which forms spreading clumps to 3m tall on forest margins, hillsides and embankments. Also colonises sandstone rocks around Sydney.

ID: Rhizomes long-creeping. Fronds 2-pinnate, arranged in tiers. Primary pinnae divided almost to the midrib into narrow segments, green to pale green above, glaucous beneath.

RANGE/HABITAT: WA (n), NT (n), Qld (n to s), NSW (ne, Sydney Basin); NZ, Af, As, Oc. Open sites in moist/wet soil.

GIANT SCRAMBLING FERN

Diplopterygium longissimum

Vigorous climbing fern, commonly seen in large, crowded, tangled clumps on exposed forest margins and road banks in the mountains. Dies out if overgrown by forest.

ID: Rhizomes long-creeping. Fronds to 6m long, bipinnate, arranged in tiers. Primary pinnae to 2m x 40cm, divided almost to the midrib into narrow segments, dark green above, glaucous beneath.

RANGE/HABITAT: Qld (Windsor Tlnd to Eungella); NG, Af, As, Oc. Sheltered slopes.

ALPINE CORAL FERN *Gleichenia alpina*

Hardy matting fern which grows in cold alpine/subalpine areas. Forms dense, tightly interwoven clumps that spread across the ground surface, often to the exclusion of other plants.

ID: Rhizomes short-creeping, 2.5mm diam., branching freely. Stipes to 40cm long, in clusters. Fronds in 1–8 tiers, to 40 x 6cm. Ultimate segments round, to 1 x 1mm, dark green, underside white and with brown scales.

RANGE/HABITAT: Tas; NZ. Heath, grassland and bogs above 800m alt.

SCRAMBLING CORAL FERN *Gleichenia microphylla*

Scrambling fern forming extensive spreading/climbing colonies on exposed slopes, embankments, swamps and trees. Stunted plants often occur in wet rock crevices.

ID: Rhizomes long-creeping, to 3.5mm diam., branching freely. Stipes to 55cm long, widely spaced along rhizomes. Fronds in 1–3 tiers, to 2m tall. Ultimate segments oblong, flat, to 2.5 x 2mm, dark green, underside pale green.

RANGE/HABITAT: NSW, Vic (s), Tas, SA (se); NZ, As, Oc. Wet soil in open forest.

UMBRELLA FERN *Sticherus flabellatus* var. *flabellatus*

Bushy fern which spreads by wiry long-creeping rhizomes to form colonies. Decorative, erect/straggling light green to yellowish fronds branch to form 1–3 tiers of pinnae which spread like an inverted umbrella.

ID: Rhizomes to 7mm diam., with brown scales Stipes to 95cm long. Fronds to 2m tall. Ultimate segments at 45º to rachis, narrow, to 45 x 4mm.

RANGE/HABITAT: Qld (n to s), NSW, Vic (e); NZ, NCal. Sheltered slopes and streambanks.

SCRAMBLING FAN FERN *Sticherus milnei*

Localised uncommon fern forming spreading tiered clumps of bright green branching fronds with comb-like segments. Tufts of deeply dissected leaflets arise at the main forks along the stem.

ID: Rhizomes long-creeping, 2.5mm diam. Stipes to 50cm long. Fronds in 2–4 tiers, branching freely. Ultimate segments at right angles to the rachis, narrow, underside pale green.

RANGE/HABITAT: Qld (n Cape York Pen.); also NG, Oc. Open forest, stream banks, springs.

New growth.

SMOOTH FINGER FERN *Notogrammitis billardierei*

HAIRY FINGER FERN *Oreogrammitis wurunuran*

Two species of small grammitid ferns with simple fronds. Often found in crowded groups on mossy tree trunks, wet rocks and tree fern trunks in wetter forests, including rainforest. Both previously placed in *Grammitis*.

◀ *N. billardierei* has smooth fronds to 16cm long. NSW, Vic, Tas; NZ.

◀ *O. wurunuran*, which is endemic in the ranges and tlnds of ne Qld, has hairy fronds to 10cm long.

GYPSY FERN *Notogrammitis heterophylla*

Decorative small fern with arching/pendulous, leathery, pinnate/pinnatifid fronds that arise from the rhizome in 2 rows. Fronds curl during dry periods, refreshing after rain. PKA *Ctenopteris heterophylla*.

ID: Rhizomes short-creeping. Stipes winged. Fronds 5–30cm x 5–10mm, dull green. Sporangia in 2 elongated sori near the apex of each frond.

RANGE/HABITAT: Vic (s), Tas.; NZ. Rocks, mossy trunks and branches in fern gullies and wetter forests.

SLING FERN *Prosaptia fuscopilosa*

Clumping fern with narrow arching/pendent, dark green, leathery, pinnate fronds. Usually seen growing on mossy granite boulders near streams; also low down on tree trunks. PKA *Ctenopteris fuscopilosa*.

ID: Rhizomes short-creeping, green with brown scales. Fronds to 30 x 2.5cm, widest near middle and tapered to each end, dull. Sori in shallow depressions.

RANGE/HABITAT: Qld (Windsor Tlnd to Ravenshoe). Endemic. Rainforest, wet sclerophyll forest.

GRUB FERN *Scleroglossum wooroonooran*

Small clumping fern growing on tree trunks and boulders in the wet forests of ne Qld. Often locally common in crowded patches on ridges and peaks where clouds and mists are frequent. Fronds become papery during dry periods.

ID: Rhizomes tufted. Fronds simple, spathulate, 1–4cm x 2–5mm, dull green. Sporangia in 2 elongated sori near each frond apex.

RANGE/HABITAT: Qld (Mt Finnigan to Mt Elliot). Endemic. Rainforest.

PROP-ROOT FERN *Abrodictyum obscurum*

Terrestrial filmy fern with woody roots that prop up the rhizome. Stiffly spreading dark olive-green fronds have a shiny lustre when wet. PKA *Cephalomanes obscurum, Selenodesmium obscurum.*

ID: Rhizomes short-creeping to erect. Fronds 3-pinnate, to 30 x 9cm (including stipes), coarse-textured. Pinnae crowded, overlapping, tips flat or curled.

RANGE/HABITAT: NT (n), Qld, NSW (Torres Strait to Richmond R.); Oc. Rainforest. Among rocks, crevices, stream banks, clay slopes.

SATIN FERN *Cephalomanes atrovirens*

Extraordinary filmy fern with spreading, dark green fronds which when wet appear to have a lustrous bluish sheen or polished glassy look.

ID: Roots black, wiry, sometimes stilt-like. Rhizomes erect. Stipes to 45mm long, dark red. Fronds to 25 x 4cm, pinnate, coarse-textured. Pinnae 1–2cm long, crowded, overlapping. Sori with a tubular indusium.

RANGE/HABITAT: Qld (Ayton to Innisfail); LHI, NG, As, Oc. Clay banks and near streams in wet lowland rainforest.

Sori.

APHLEBIAE FERN *Crepidomanes aphlebioides*

Spectacular filmy fern readily recognised by its relatively thick rhizomes which carry small deeply dissected fronds (1–20mm long, termed aphlebiae) hidden among the stipes of the true fronds. Rare sp. known from few localities.

ID: Rhizomes long-creeping, 2–3mm diam, hairy. Fronds to 90cm long (including black stipe), 30cm wide, 4-pinnate/pinnatifid, dark green.

RANGE/HABITAT: Qld (Daintree region, Captain Billy Landing); also NG, As, Oc. Steep banks in wet lowland rainforest.

FAN FILMY FERN *Crepidomanes saxifragoides*

GLOB FERN *Didymoglossum tahitense*

Two morphologically distinct filmy ferns that grow on wet mossy rocks and tree trunks in rainforest. Both previously placed in *Trichomanes*.

◀ *C. saxifragoides* forms dense mats with branching thread-like rhizomes and small, dark green, fan-shaped fronds with urn-like marginal indusia. Qld, NSW; NFK, CI, As. Oc.

◀ *D. tahitense* has thin rhizomes covered with black hairs and strings of dark green, shiny, flat, circular, glob-like fronds with prominent radiating lines (false veins). Qld (ne); As, Oc.

PALE FILMY FERN *Hymenophyllum flabellatum*

SLENDER FILMY FERN *Hymenophyllum rarum*

Two similar filmy ferns that may grow together. Both have a narrow hanging fronds to c.16cm long and grow on mossy tree trunks, wet rocks and tree fern trunks in wet fern gullies and rainforest.

◄ *H. flabellatum* has scattered hairs on the stipes and relatively broad, pale green, crowded fronds. Qld (n to s), NSW, Vic (s), Tas); Oc.

◄ *H. rarum* has glabrous stipes and narrower, less dissected, dark green fronds. NSW, Vic (s), Tas; Oc.

PALE FILMY FERN *Hymenophyllum pallidum*

ALPINE FILMY FERN *Hymenophyllum peltatum*

Two related but very different filmy ferns that grow on wet mossy rocks and tree trunks in vastly different habitats.

◀ *H. pallidum* from tropical rainforest has broad, waxy, grey-bluish fronds with pale brown hairs. Qld (Thornton Ra. to Kirrima Ra.); As, Oc.

◀ *H. peltatum*, commonest in cool temperate rainforest and often growing on Myrtle Beech, has narrow dark green fronds with toothed margins. Qld (rare in se), NSW, Vic, Tas: NZ, As, Oc.

GUNN'S QUILLWORT *Isoetes gunnii*

Aquatic lycophyte growing in shallow water and rooting in mud. Dark green, rigid, cylindrical leaves are arranged spirally in a crowded tuft. Often massed on the margins of still waterways. Uprooted and eaten by waterfowl.

ID: Stem (corm) 3–4cm wide, 3-lobed. Leaves to 60 per plant, erect/recurved, to 18 x 0.5cm, base broadly expanded, white with brownish margins. Sporangia not covered by a veil.

RANGE/HABITAT: Tas. Endemic. Alpine and subalpine lakes.

LOBED SWORD FERN *Lindsaea agatii*

Coarse, clumping terrestrial fern that grows in localised patches. Similar to *L. ensifolia* but distinguished by the small, lobed terminal pinna and the lower pinnae being pinnately divided.

ID: Rhizomes creeping. Stipes wiry, brown/black. Fronds monomorphic, 1–2-pinnate, to 80cm tall, pale green/yellowish, somewhat leathery.

RANGE/HABITAT: NT (n), Qld (n to s); Oc. Open forest and swamp margins.

SHORT-FOOTED SCREW FERN

Lindsaea brachypoda

Delicate fern that grows on mossy rocks and moist earth banks in rainforest, usually in humid gullies and near streams. The narrow pinnate fronds, which arise in tufts, spread widely but are usually appressed close to the supporting host.

ID: Rhizomes short-creeping. Stipes clustered. Fronds dimorphic, bright green. Fertile fronds to 30 x 2cm. Sterile fronds shorter. Lower pinnae decurved.

RANGE/HABITAT: NT (n), Qld, NSW (Thursday Is. to Minyon Falls). Endemic.

SLENDER SCREW FERN *Lindsaea incisa*

SCREW FERN *Lindsaea linearis*

Two spp. of small terrestrial ferns with narrow fronds. Both grow in open forest and heath, *L. incisa* often in damp to wet soils.

◀ *L. incisa* has bright green, monomorphic, 1–2-pinnate fronds to 40 x 1.5cm with the pinnae margins incised. Qld, NSW (Mt Fox to Corindi). Endemic.

◀ *L. linearis* has short sterile fronds in a basal group around taller fertile fronds (to 25cm tall). Qld (se), NSW, Vic (s), Tas, SA, WA (sw); NFK, NCal, NZ.

LACY WEDGE FERN *Lindsaea microphylla*

Decorative fern that is much tougher than its delicate appearance suggests. Readily recognised by its crowded clumps of finely divided, yellowish-green, lacy fronds. Often on clay banks, embankments and track margins. Regrows well after fire.

ID: Rhizomes short-creeping. Stipes clustered. Fronds monomorphic, crowded, 2–3-pinnate, to 50 x 6cm.

RANGE/HABITAT: Qld (n to Daintree), NSW, Vic (se). Endemic. Coast to mountains in damp soil in forest and rainforest margins.

CLIMBING WEDGE FERN *Lindsaea repens*

High-climbing fern with thin wiry rhizomes and widely spaced bright green, erect to pendulous monomorphic fronds.

ID: Rhizomes scandent, thin, scaly. Stipes pale brown. Fronds to 75 x 6cm (including short stipe), thin textured, bright green. Pinnae crowded, spreading widely, to 30 x 7mm, longest in centre of frond, upper margin shallowly toothed. Frond apex pinnatifid.

RANGE/HABITAT: Qld (sporadically from Iron Ra. to Fraser Is.); Af, As, Oc. Sheltered sites in very wet forests; mainly low alt.

Climbing.

OVAL WEDGE FERN *Lindsaea trichomanoides*

Uncommon/rare fern that grows as a terrestrial, on rotting logs and occas. on the base of tree trunks. Usually in dense shade on steep slopes in deep gullies and near streams.

ID: Rhizomes short- to medium-creeping. Stipes clustered or spaced. Fronds monomorphic, dark green, 1–2-pinnate, to 20 x 6cm.

RANGE/HABITAT: NSW (s from Blue Mtns), Vic (Gippsland), Tas (w, sw); NZ. Wetter forests, including rainforest.

KING'S CLIMBING FERN *Lomariopsis kingii*

High-climbing fern with a thick, woody rhizome and dimorphic pinnate fronds which vary in shape and division. Fertile fronds smaller than sterile fronds. Juvenile fronds simple. Occas. grows as a terrestrial.

ID: Rhizomes scandent, c.1cm thick. Stipe 6–20cm long, base scaly. Sterile fronds to 50cm long, erect/pendulous, leathery, dark green, paler beneath. Sterile pinnae to 3cm wide, fertile pinnae c.2mm wide.

RANGE/HABITAT: Qld (Ayton to Innisfail); Oc. Low-altitude rainforest.

Juvenile fronds.

MOUNTAIN CLUBMOSS
Austrolycopodium fastigiatum

SPREADING CLUBMOSS *Diphasium scariosum*

Two similar lycophytes with spreading to upright branching stems clothed with small leaves and terminal strobili projecting above the foliage. Both species grow in alpine/subalpine areas and extend onto Subantarctic islands.

◀ *A. fastigiatum* has spirally arranged, thin, overlapping, green to yellow/orange leaves. NSW (se), Vic, Tas; NZ.

◀ *D. scariosum* has two types of rigid, yellowish green leaves in flattish rows, leaves on upper surface of stems larger than those on lower surface. Vic, Tas; NZ.

SCRAMBLING CLUBMOSS *Palhinhaea cernua*

Vigorous lycophyte that scrambles through shrubs and other vegetation, sometimes covering large areas. Arching/drooping branchlets carry clusters of small green to yellowish, forward-curving leaves and compact whitish strobili on the tips. PKA *Lycopodium cernuum, Lycopodiella cernua.*

ID: Stems 0.3–2m tall. Leaves 1.5–4.5 x 0.3–1mm. Strobili 5–15mm long.

RANGE/HABITAT: WA (n), NT (n), Qld, NSW (Torres Strait to Heathcote); LHI, NFK, Af, As, Oc. Open sites and forest margins in wettish soil.

KEELED TASSELL FERN *Phlegmariurus carinatus*

Rare pale grey-green clumping lycophyte with branched arching/pendulous stems. Leaves in 4 rows, strongly keeled, pointing forwards and held close to stem. Transition from sterile to fertile zone gradual. Spore-bearing zone apical, sparsely branched. PKA *Lycopodium carinatum, Huperzia carinata.*

ID: Stems to 80cm long. Leaves 10–13 x 1–2mm, leathery, pointed. Fertile leaflets 4–8 x 1–2.5mm.

RANGE/HABITAT: Qld (Iron Ra., McIlwraith Ra.); As, Oc. Trees in wet tropical rainforest.

BLUE TASSELL FERN *Phlegmariurus dalhousieanus*

Rare clumping lycophyte growing in clumps of *Platycerium hillii*. Stems arching/pendulous, sparsely branched. Leaves blue-grey, crowded in whorls of 3, at c.45º to the stem, pointed. Transition from sterile to fertile zone gradual. Spore-bearing zone apical, short, unbranched or 1-forked. PKA *Lycopodium dalhousieanum, Huperzia dalhousieana*.

ID: Stems to 120cm long. Leaves 15–25 x 3–4mm. Fertile leaflets 10–20 x 1.5–2mm.

RANGE/HABITAT: Qld (McIlwraith Ra. to Tully); NG, As, Oc. Rainforest and vine forest.

COARSE TASSELL FERN *Phlegmariurus harmsii*

Clumping lycophyte with arching/pendulous branching stems. Leaves crowded, dark green, shiny, spreading at c.50º to the stem, twisted at base, pointed. Transition from sterile to fertile zone sudden. Spore-bearing tassells 10–30 x 2.5mm, 1–6-forked.

ID: Stems to 180cm long. Leaves 10–25 x 4–8mm. Fertile leaflets 1–2 x 1–1.5mm.

RANGE/HABITAT: Qld (Captain Billy Landing to Eungella); CI, As, Oc. Rocks and trees in mangroves and rainforest.

ROCK TASSELL FERN *Phlegmariurus squarrosus*

Rare clumping lycophyte with branched arching/pendulous stems. Leaves dark green to yellow-green, crowded, at c.70º to the stem, narrow, twisted near base, pointed. Transition from sterile to fertile zone gradual. Spore-bearing zone 10–30 x 1cm, unbranched or 1-forked. PKA *Lycopodium squarrosum, Huperzia squarrosa.*

ID: Stems to 75cm long. Leaves 10–20 x 1–2mm. Fertile leaflets 5–7 x 1.5–2mm.

RANGE/HABITAT: Qld (Daintree to Tully); As, Oc. Rocks and trees near streams in rainforest.

GIANT SNAKE FERN *Lygodium reticulatum*

Robust high-climbing fern with thin rhizomes and long wiry climbing rachises that twine around supports. Fronds are pinnate, in pairs on secondary branches, each frond divided into stalked leaflets.

ID: Rhizomes long-creeping. Pinnae to 20 x 16cm. Leaflets to 14 x 3cm, leathery, dark green. Fertile leaflets with marginal sporangia to 7mm long.

RANGE/HABITAT: Qld (Cape York to Yeppoon); Oc. Forest margins, road embankments.

Fertile leaflets.

KING FERN, GIANT FERN *Angiopteris evecta*

Large fern with a massive fleshy trunk (to 1m diam. in old plants) and long arching fronds. The frond stalks contain no strengthening tissue and sag/flop in dry times, reinvigorating after rain.

ID: Frond bases enclosed by a pair of ear-like stipules. Stipes to 2m long, smooth, green. Fronds to 9 x 2.5m, bipinnate, dark green, shiny.

RANGE/HABITAT: NT (Arnhem Land), Qld (McIlwraith Ra. to Eungella, se), NSW (1 plant); NG, As, Oc. Wetter forests.

Trunk.

Crozier.

POTATO FERN *Ptisana oreades*

Large fern with a fleshy trunk to 50cm diam. in old plants and broad arching fronds. The frond stalks contain no strengthening tissue and sag/flop in dry times. PKA *Marattia oreades*.

ID: Frond bases enclosed by a pair of ear-like stipules. Stipes to 75cm long, rough, green. Fronds to 4 x 1m, bipinnate, dark green, shiny.

RANGE/HABITAT: Qld (McIlwraith Ra. to Eungella, se). Endemic. Slopes and streambanks in rainforest.

Sporangia.

COMMON NARDOO *Marsilea drummondii*

Robust aquatic or terrestrial fern with freely branching hairy rhizomes and fronds with hairy leaflets arranged like a 4-leaved clover. Forms crowded spreading clumps in wet soil, mud or shallow water with floating or emergent fronds.

ID: Fronds to 30cm long, clustered. Leaflets to 35 x 10mm, broadly wedge-shaped, evenly spreading. Sporocarps hairy.

RANGE/HABITAT: Inland areas of all mainland states. Endemic. Wet depressions, swamps, still or sluggish water.

Sporocarps.

SMOOTH NARDOO *Marsilea mutica*

Common aquatic fern with hairless rhizomes growing through mud and shiny, smooth fronds floating on the surface. New fronds have a central green area surrounded by a brownish outer zone. Unusually the fronds close at night (photo).

ID: Fronds to 90cm long, single. Leaflets to 50 x 40mm, broadly wedge-shaped, overlapping. Sporocarps hairy.

RANGE/HABITAT: Near-coastal WA (n), NT, Qld, NSW, ACT, Vic, Tas (s); NCal. Swamps, lakes, billabongs, still or sluggish water.

Fronds closed at night.

WOOLLY FISHBONE FERN *Nephrolepis acutifolia*

Robust clumping fern mainly found among boulders and rock faces. Also colonises large elkhorn clumps and leaf bases of palms. Woolly when young, the leathery pale grey-green fronds have spreading pinnae with prominent white pores along the margins.

ID: Rhizomes tufted. Runners numerous. Fronds dimorphic, 1-pinnate, to 1.5m long. Sterile pinnae blunt, fertile pinnae longer, pointed.

RANGE/HABITAT: WA (nw), NT (n), Qld (Iron Ra. to Gladstone); Af, As, Oc. Rockpile vegetation, palm swamps, mangroves, littoral rainforest.

GORGE FERN *Nephrolepis arida*

Specialised fern colonising wet crevices, ledges and seepage sites in sheltered sandstone gorges surrounded by arid desert vegetation. Fronds pinnate, arching/hanging, light green to bright green. Forms small patches that spread by numerous runners.

ID: Rhizomes tufted. Runners slender. Fronds to 1.7m x 9cm. Sterile and fertile pinnae similar, fertile pinnae slightly longer and narrower.

RANGE/HABITAT: WA (nw), NT (nw and Talliputta Gorge). Endemic. Sandstone gorges.

GIANT FISHBONE FERN *Nephrolepis biserrata*

Large, vigorous fern that grows in tangled colonies in bright sun or lightly shaded areas. Often among rocks. Mainly coastal/near-coastal areas but also hinterland streambanks and some inland gorges.

ID: Rhizomes tufted. Fronds 1-pinnate, to 2.5m long, dark green, bleached in sun. Fertile pinnae longer (to 24cm) than sterile pinnae (to 12cm) and with deeply notched margins.

RANGE/HABITAT: WA (nw), NT (n), Qld (S to Bowen); CI, pantropical. Rainforest margins, monsoon forest, open forest.

FISHBONE FERN, HERRINGBONE FERN

Nephrolepis cordifolia

Although native to eastern Aust., this familiar garden fern is now widely naturalised and treated as an environmental weed in Qld and NSW. Fleshy tubers develop on the roots of plants from some areas.

ID: Rhizomes tufted. Fronds 1-pinnate, to 1m x 7cm, pale green. Sterile and fertile pinnae similar in size and shape.

RANGE/HABITAT: Qld (Cooktown to Clarence R.); pantropical. Rainforest and open forest, often among rocks.

Cultivated.

STILT FERN *Oleandra musifolia*

The attractively patterned rhizomes of this sprawling/clumping fern are held above the host on long, wiry, stilt-like aerial roots. Often found in clumps of other epiphytes, this distinctive fern can also climb trees.

ID: Rhizomes long-creeping, to 5mm diam., covered with red-brown scales. Stipes to 20mm long, in clusters. Fronds simple, to 50cm long, pale green, thin textured/papery.

RANGE/HABITAT: Qld (Windsor Tlnd to Eungella); also NG, As, Oc. Earth banks, trees, rocks in wetter forests, including rainforest.

MOONWORT *Botrychium lunaria*

Resprouting terrestrial fern with a narrow, pinnate sterile frond and fertile structures (sporophores) that resemble strings of green grapes (brown with age). Rarely seen sp. Dormant in winter.

ID: Fronds 3–18cm tall. Sterile blade to 7 x 2.5cm, ±oblong, 1-pinnate, green. Fertile blade longer than sterile blade, carried on its own thick stipe.

RANGE/HABITAT: NSW (se), ACT, Vic (e), Tas; Europe, Asia, America. Grassland and open grassy forest above 700m alt.

FLOWERING FERN *Helminthostachys zeylanica*

Resprouting terrestrial fern that grows in thick layers of litter, peat and alluvial soil. Dormant in dry season.

ID: Frond with a common basal stalk to 40cm long; main sterile segments 3, to 20cm x 40mm, each divided into 3 or 5 dark green leaflets. Sporophore cylindrical, to 13cm x 10mm, green, on stipe of similar length.

RANGE/HABITAT: Tropical Qld, NT, WA; NG, As, Oc. Coastal scrubs, swamp forest, vine thickets.

RIBBON FERN *Ophioderma pendula*

Evergreen epiphytic fern that commonly germinates and grows in the clumps of bulky epiphytes, particularly elkhorns and bird's nest ferns. PKA *Ophioglossum pendulum*.

ID: Rhizomes short-creeping, white, fleshy. Fronds in clusters, to 2m x 3cm, pendulous, fleshy, bright green, often weakly twisted, simple or forked. Sporophore carried on flat stipe, to 30cm x 15mm, pendent, sausage-like, fleshy.

RANGE/HABITAT: Qld, NSW (Torres Strait Is. to Milton); LHI, CI, As, Oc. Coast to tlnds in rainforest.

Sporophores.

AUSTRAL ADDER'S TONGUE

Ophioglossum lusitanicum

Colonial resprouting terrestrial fern with simple, leaf-like fronds (often tongue-shaped) and an erect green sporophore on a short stipe. Fleshy roots proliferate to produce new plantlets. Dormant in winter. PKA *Ophioglossum coriaceum*.

ID: Sterile blade to 75 x 15mm, ovate, fleshy, green. Sporophore to 15mm long, spike-like, on stipe to 10cm long.

RANGE/HABITAT: Qld (s), NSW, ACT, Vic, Tas, SA, WA, NT (s); worldwide. Moisture-retentive soil in grassy, shrubby and forested habitats.

AUSTRAL MOONWORT, PARSLEY FERN

Sceptridium australe

Resprouting terrestrial fern with contractile roots, a sterile frond that resemble a parsley leaf and a longer fertile structure that resembles a bunch of green grapes (brown with age). Dormant in winter. PKA *Botrychium australe*.

ID: Fronds 5–50cm tall. Sterile blade to 22 x 25cm, ±triangular, 3-pinnate, green to yellow-green.

RANGE/HABITAT: Qld (n to s), NSW, ACT, Vic, Tas (rare), SA (extinct); LHI, NZ, NG. Lowlands to mountains in open forest, grassland and rainforest.

CREPE FERN *Leptopteris fraseri*

Handsome fern which grows on or among rocks in constantly wet sheltered gullies, caves and waterfalls. Extends to 1,600m alt on mountain tops in ne Qld. Very sensitive to dryness.

ID: Rhizomes erect, in old plants a naked, woody trunk to 1m tall. Stipes to 45cm long, shiny. Fronds membranous, dark green-bluish, translucent, in a spreading/arching crown, 2–3-pinnate/pinnatifid, to 100 x 32cm.

RANGE/HABITAT: Qld (ne), NSW (Walcha to Bundanoon). Endemic. Rainforest.

Sporelings.

KING FERN *Todea barbara*

Imposing fern with a multi-headed crown topping a black fibrous trunk. Often forms extensive patches in wet sheltered areas. Occas. stunted plants occur in rock crevices. Mature spores are green.

ID: Rhizomes erect, to 3 x 2m in old plants. Fronds erect to arching, leathery, dark green, to 2.5m x 60cm, 1–2-pinnate.

RANGE/HABITAT: Qld (n to Windsor Tlnd), NSW, Vic, Tas, SA (se); NZ, Af, Oc. Swamps, streambanks, gullies.

Juvenile plant.

NETTED FERN *Dendroconche ampla*

Climbing or scrambling fern. Rhizome broad, flattish. Stipes winged. Decorative dark green, shiny, thin-textured fronds with conspicuous netted veins are either undivided or pinnately lobed. PKA *Colysis ampla*.

ID: Rhizomes creeping, flattish, densely scaly. Fronds to 80 x 40cm (including stipe).

RANGE/HABITAT: Qld (McIlwraith Ra. to Paluma). Endemic. Coast to mountains on rocks and small trees in rainforest, often near streams.

FRAGRANT FERN *Dendroconche scandens*

Scrambling fern that forms impressive patches of foliage on rocks, trees and tree fern trunks. Fresh fronds have a musky scent (not discernable to some people). PKA *Microsorum scandens*.

ID: Rhizomes long-creeping, wiry, densely scaly. Fronds either simple and undivided (to 40 x 3cm) or pinnately lobed (to 60 x 20cm) (including stipe), dark green, thin textured.

RANGE/HABITAT: Qld (n to Mossman Gorge), NSW, Vic (se); LHI, NZ. Rainforest.

STRAP FERN *Dictymia brownii*

Clumping epiphyte which grows into large, crowded clumps on rocks or trees. Simple, dark green, strap-like fronds have smooth or wavy margins and large, brown, elliptic/rounded sori sunken in the undersurface.

ID: Rhizomes long-creeping, to 6cm diam., with dark scales. Sterile and fertile fronds of similar shape and size, to 90 x 2cm.

RANGE/HABITAT: Qld, NSW (Windsor Tlnd to Blue Mtns, Batlow). Endemic. Wetter forests, including rainforest.

OAKLEAF FERN *Drynaria quercifolia*

Robust colony-forming fern with thick, creeping, woolly rhizomes and dimorphic fronds. Sterile fronds upright, lobed. Foliage fronds pinnatifid, pale green, the pinnae bases running along the main frond axis. Spreading patches on rock faces, among boulders and on trees. Fertile fronds die off in dry times.

ID: Rhizomes long-creeping, to 2cm diam., brown. Nest fronds to 40 x 25cm. Foliage fronds to 100 x 50cm.

RANGE/HABITAT: Tropical Qld, NT, WA; NG, As, Oc. Rainforest margins, open forest.

BASKET FERN *Drynaria rigidula*

Common vigorous fern with dimorphic fronds. Often forms basket-like clumps in trees with the upright nest fronds catching forest litter and the foliage fronds forming an overhead cover. Also spreading patches on rock faces and earthen banks.

ID: Rhizomes long-creeping, to 1cm diam. Nest fronds to 40 x 14cm. Foliage fronds 1-pinnate, to 200 x 50cm, dark green, leathery.

RANGE/HABITAT: Qld, NSW (McIlwraith Ra. to Clarence R.); As, Oc. Rainforest margins, sheltered rock outcrops.

Nest fronds.

GLOSSY WEEPING FERN *Goniophlebium percussum*

Decorative clumping epiphyte with pendulous glossy bright green pinnate fronds. Rounded sori appear as raised bumps on the upper surface of fertile pinnae. Often grows in clumps of other epiphytes.

ID: Rhizomes creeping, greenish, fleshy. Sterile and fertile fronds similar in size/shape, to 2m x 40cm. Pinnae 3–5cm apart, stalked, to 20 x 3cm, apex pointed.

RANGE/HABITAT: Qld (Cooktown to Bowen); NG, As, Oc. Trees and palms in wetter forests and swamps.

CHALKSTICK FERN *Goniophlebium percussum*

The chalky white surface of older rhizomes is a useful means of recognising this decorative epiphytic fern which has arching/weeping dull pale green pinnate fronds. Often grows in clumps of other epiphytes. Occas. earthen banks.

ID: Rhizomes creeping. Sterile and fertile fronds similar in size/shape, to 1.2m x 40cm. Pinnae 1–2.5cm apart, stalked, to 25 x 2cm, margins toothed, apex pointed.

RANGE/HABITAT: Qld (Iron Ra. to Eungella); NG, As, Oc. Rainforest, swamps.

Sori.

FALSE NEST FERN *Microsorum australiense*

Superficially similar to some nest-forming spp. of *Asplenium* but with a creeping rhizome and small round sori. Narrow bright green to bluish-green fronds are widest near the middle and taper to each end, apex pointed.

ID: Rhizomes short-creeping, flattish, green, fleshy with dark scales. Sterile and fertile fronds similar in size/shape, to 50 x 4cm.

RANGE/HABITAT: Qld (Mt Finnigan to Paluma Ra.). Endemic. Trees and rocks in rainforest.

CLOVEN FERN *Microsorum grossum*

Usually growing in the ground, this fern forms spreading patches in rainforest and in sand in coastal scrub. Upright bright green to bluish-green deeply lobed fronds have up to 30 lobes per frond.

ID: Rhizomes long-creeping, flattish, green, fleshy, scaly when young. Fronds to 190 x 40cm (including stipe).

RANGE/HABITAT: WA (nw), NT (n), Qld (Torres Strait Is. to Stradbroke Is.); NG, Oc.

Sori.

PIMPLE FERN *Microsorum membranifolium*

Easily recognised by the prominent pimple-like bumps on the upper surface of the fronds, the bumps corresponding with the rounded, sunken sori on the lower surface. Forms spreading clumps on rocks and trees.

ID: Rhizomes short-creeping, pale green, fleshy. Fronds to 120 x 60cm (including stipe), pinnately lobed, dark green, leathery.

RANGE/HABITAT: Qld (Daintree to Babinda); Oc. Coast to mountains in rainforest.

CREEPING STRAP FERN *Microsorum punctatum*

Vigorous fern that forms spreading colonies on rocks, boulders and in sandy soil, often in situations of bright light or filtered sunshine. Tolerant of lengthy dry spells.

ID: Rhizomes short to long-creeping, flattish, green, fleshy. Fronds simple, undivided, to 1.5m x 11cm, green to yellow-green, broadest near middle, tapered to rounded apex.

RANGE/HABITAT: Qld (Torres Strait Is. to Stradbroke Is.); Af, As, Oc. Monsoon forests, rockpile vegetation, beach scrubs, rainforest.

ELKHORN *Platycerium bifurcatum*

Common epiphytic fern forming small to large spreading clumps on trees, cliff faces and boulders. Fronds strongly dimorphic. Sterile fronds (nest leaves) collect litter. Foliage fronds produce spores.

ID: Nest leaves upright, lobed. Foliage fronds erect to pendulous, tips drooping, upper surface green, undersurface greyish, irregularly forked 2–5-times, lower surface covered with brown sporangia.

RANGE/HABITAT: Qld, NSW (Cooktown to Mimosa Rocks); LHI. Endemic. Coast to mountains in wetter forests.

NORTHERN ELKHORN *Platycerium hillii*

Bulky epiphytic fern forming small to large rounded to spreading clumps on trees and rocks. Fronds strongly dimorphic. Sterile fronds (nest leaves) collect litter. Foliage fronds produce spores.

ID: Nest leaves closely incurved, green ageing brown, margins entire. Foliage fronds erect to spreading, both surfaces green, irregularly forked 1–5-times, underside of tips covered with brown sporangia.

RANGE/HABITAT: Qld (Iron Ra. to Cape Hillsborough). Endemic. Coastal scrubs, vine thickets, lowland rainforest.

STAGHORN *Platycerium superbum*

Distinctive large epiphytic fern that that enlarges each year as a single clump. Fronds strongly dimorphic. Sterile fronds (nest leaves) collect litter. Foliage fronds produce spores.

ID: Nest leaves silvery-grey, spreading, incurved with age, deeply forked. Foliage fronds usually in pairs, to 2m long, pendulous, both surfaces green, irregularly forked 4–6-times. Large brown patch of sporangia on underside of first fork.

RANGE/HABITAT: Qld, NSW (Windsor Tlnd to Nabiac). Endemic. Trees and rocks in wetter forests.

SILVER ELKHORN *Platycerium veitchii*

Dryness-tolerant clumping fern usually found on rocks, occas. on Hoop Pines. Fronds strongly dimorphic. Sterile fronds (nest leaves) collect litter. Foliage fronds produce spores. Distributed sporadically from near coast to isolated western areas.

ID: Whole plant silvery grey. Nest leaves deeply lobed into narrow segments. Foliage fronds erect, irregularly forked 1–4-times, lower surface densely covered with white hairs, often masking the sporangia.

RANGE/HABITAT: Qld (Mount Carbine to Carnarvon). Endemic. Monsoon forest, vine thickets.

ROCK FELT FERN *Pyrrosia rupestris*

Common matting fern growing in sheltered humid places, often among clumps of other epiphytes. Dimorphic fronds curl and shrivel in dry times, refreshing after rain.

ID: Rhizomes thin, long-creeping. Sterile fronds round to elongate, green to rust coloured. Fertile fronds to 20cm long, mixed with sterile fronds, numerous small brown sori on underside.

RANGE/HABITAT: Qld, NSW, ACT, Vic (Mt Finnigan to Mt Drummer); NG, Oc. Coast to mtns on rocks and trees in wetter forests.

Juvenile fronds.

GINGERFOOT FERN *Selliguea simplicissima*

Creeping fern with thin, densely scaly rhizomes and widely spaced, simple, undivided narrow fronds variable in size and shape. Common on rocks, boulders and trees. PKA *Crypsinus simplicissimus*.

ID: Rhizomes long-creeping, thin, covered with ginger scales. Sterile fronds to 15 x 2.8cm, fertile fronds to 25 x 1.5cm, margins entire or bluntly toothed, apex in an extended point.

RANGE/HABITAT: Qld (Mt Finnigan to Mt Elliot). Endemic. Coast to mountains in wetter forests.

KANGAROO FERN *Zealandia pustulata*

Scrambling fern with pale green to yellowish, simple or lobed fronds. Colonises rocky surfaces, tree trunks and the fibrous trunks of tree ferns, occas. even as a terrestrial in the ground. PKA *Microsorum pustulatum, M. diversifolium.*

ID: Rhizomes long-creeping, fleshy, green or glaucous. Fronds simple (to 30 x 3cm) or pinnately lobed (to 50 x 30cm, including stipe), leathery.

RANGE/HABITAT: Qld (se), NSW, ACT, Vic (s), Tas; NFK, NZ. Wetter forests.

SKELETON FORK FERN, WHISK FERN

Psilotum nudum

Weedy epiphyte that lacks leaves and roots and hardly resembles a fern. Occurs naturally in crevices, palms, trees, other epiphyte clumps and earthen banks. Often naturalises in urban areas, greenhouses and gardens. Spores produced in a specialised synganium.

ID: Rhizomes branched, creeping/clumping. Aerial shoots to 85cm long, skeleton-like, forking repeatedly, dark green to yellow, ribbed. Syngania yellow when mature.

RANGE/HABITAT: Qld (n to s), NSW, Vic (e), WA (s), NT (s); LHI, NFK, Af, As, Oc.

In rock.

LONG FORK FERN *Tmesipteris elongata*

OVATE FORK FERN *Tmesipteris ovata*

Two similar epiphytes that may grow together. Both have narrow hanging growths, similar spirally arranged dark green leaf-like structures with the rhizomes buried in the fibrous trunks of Soft Tree Fern. Spores are produced in syngania.

◀ *T. elongata* has growths to 40cm long and 'leaves' to 26 x 5mm. Qld, NSW, Vic; NZ.

◀ *T. ovata* is smaller with growths to 20cm long and crowded 'leaves' to 14 x 3.5mm. Vic, Tas; NZ.

GOLDEN MANGROVE FERN *Acrostichum aureum*

Distinctive fern with coarse leathery green to golden-green fronds. Grows in saline soils, sometimes in brackish water, and commonly forms dense thickets. Rusty brown to reddish sporangia cover the whole lower surface of the fertile pinnae.

ID: Rhizomes short-creeping, stout, with thick fleshy prop roots. Fronds pinnate, 2–4m tall, erect/arching.

RANGE/HABITAT: NT (near Darwin), Qld (Torres Strait to Cardwell); Af, As, Oc. Salt marshes, mangroves, estuaries, stream banks.

Colony.

COMMON MAIDENHAIR FERN

Adiantum aethiopicum

Widespread familiar fern that spreads by wiry stolons to form mats and localised colonies. Favours moist earthen banks, seepage sites and open rocky areas.

ID: Rhizomes creeping. Scales transparent yellow, margins with no hairs. Stipes glabrous, red-brown, shiny. Fronds crowded, 2–4-pinnate, to 80 x 20cm (including stipe), triangular.

RANGE/HABITAT: NT (n), Qld (rare in ne, mainly s of Cardwell), NSW, ACT, Vic, Tas, SA; LHI, NZ, Af. Open forest, wet slopes, stream banks.

NORTHERN MAIDENHAIR FERN

Adiantum atroviride

Similar to *A. aethiopicum* but more common in the tropics. Differs by its opaque, dark brown scales with hairy margins and blackish stipes with glandular hairs. The plants often lack stolons and don't spread as widely as *A. aethiopicum*.

ID: Rhizomes erect to creeping. Fronds crowded, 2–4-pinnate, to 75 x 30cm (including stipe), triangular.

RANGE/HABITAT: NT (ne), Qld, NSW (Torres Strait to Heathcote), ?Vic; LHI. Gorges, springs, roadsides, streambanks in rainforest.

VENUS HAIR FERN *Adiantum capillus-veneris*

Although widely distributed, this delicate cosmopolitan fern is of uncommon sporadic occurrence in Australia. It mainly grows as a lithophyte with hanging fronds on wet to dripping limestone or sandstone cliffs in inland gorges, occas. as a terrestrial in calcareous soil.

ID: Rhizomes short-creeping. Stipes black, shiny. Fronds in clumps, 2–3-pinnate, to 20 x 15cm, pale green, membranous. Pinnules deeply lobed. Soral flaps not incised.

RANGE/HABITAT: All states except ACT and Tas; Af, As, Oc.

BLACK STEM, GIANT MAIDENHAIR

Adiantum formosum

Decorative fern with deeply buried rhizomes that branch freely to form spreading colonies. The main frond rachis is broadly zigzagged with the main branches arising alternately along its length.

ID: Rhizomes long-creeping, to 10cm diam. Stipes to 90cm long, black. Fronds 2–4-pinnate, to 180 x 90cm (including stipe), broadly triangular, pale green to dark green.

RANGE/HABITAT: Qld (n to Bowen, disjunct at Eungella), NSW, Vic (e); NZ. Alluvial flats in wetter forest.

SLENDER MAIDENHAIR *Adiantum philippense*

Resprouting fern which sheds its fronds in late summer/winter, regrowing in the wet season. Arching/hanging, narrow, pale green pinnate fronds arise from rock faces or crevices. Localised patches develop from plantlets on the frond tips.

ID: Rhizomes short-creeping, erect. Stipes to 15cm long, black. Fronds to 40 x 6cm (including stipe), membranous. Pinnules shallowly lobed.

RANGE/HABITAT: Tropical n. parts of Qld, NT, WA; Af, As, Oc. Springs, gorges, wet banks, often among rocks.

FOREST MAIDENHAIR *Adiantum silvaticum*

Decorative fern which forms compact clumps on earthen/clay banks on the margins of rainforest and sheltered cliffs. Occas. also a lithophyte on sandstone rock faces. Bright pink new fronds contrast with dark bluish-green mature fronds.

ID: Rhizomes short-creeping, golden denticulate scales. Stipes to 65cm long, red-brown to black. Fronds 2–3-pinnate, to 95 x 30cm (including stipe).

RANGE/HABITAT: Qld, NSW (Windsor Tlnd to Ulladulla). Endemic. Wetter forests.

New fronds.

SMALL TONGUE FERN

Antrophyum austroqueenslandicum

Extremely rare small fern that grows in groups on sheltered mossy boulders and low down on the mossy trunks of trees.

ID: Fronds simple, upright to pendent, with narrowly winged stem to 7cm long and narrow blade to 8 x 1cm, leathery, dark green, shiny, paler beneath, tapered to each end, apex bluntish. Sterile fronds shorter than fertile fronds and with broad blunt apex.

RANGE/HABITAT: Qld (Lamington NP), NSW (Border Ra.). Endemic. Highland rainforest.

OX-TONGUE FERN *Antrophyum callifolium*

Unusual tough fern which grows on boulders and trees in shady, humid, seasonally dry sites. Fronds become papery and curl during dry periods, reviving after rain.

ID: Fronds simple, pendent, to 45 x 6cm, no stipe, tongue-shaped, tapered to each end, leathery, green and shiny above, paler and dull beneath, often wrinkled.

RANGE/HABITAT: Qld (Torres Strait Is to Mackay); NG, As, Oc. Coast to ranges and tlnds in rainforest.

PADDLE FERN *Antrophyum plantagineum*

The paddle-shaped leathery fronds of this uncommon epiphytic fern curl and shrivel in dry times, refreshing after rain. Grows on boulders and trees in seasonally dry but humid, shady sites.

ID: Fronds simple, pendent, dark green, with distinct stipe to 10cm long, abruptly expanded into a blade to 20 x 8cm, tapered to pointed apex.

RANGE/HABITAT: Qld (Torres Strait Is. to Innisfail); NG, As, Oc. Coast to ranges and tlnds in rainforest.

WESTERN LIP FERN *Cheilanthes adiantoides*

Although of delicate appearance, this fern avoids dryness by dying back before the heat of summer. The infertile fronds resemble those of a maidenhair fern, but the fertile fronds have strongly inrolled margins.

ID: Fertile fronds to 25 x 9cm, 2–3-pinnate at base, 1–2-pinnate distally. Pinnules bright green, veins conspicuous. Sterile pinnules broader than fertile pinnules, margins flat.

RANGE/HABITAT: WA (widespread n of Perth). Endemic. Granite outcrops, run-off areas, moist banks.

ROCK FERN *Cheilanthes austrotenuifolia*

Widespread fern that forms patches of bright green foliage in winter/spring, dying back to its rootstock to avoid the heat and dryness of summer.

ID: Fertile fronds to 55 x 20cm, 3–4-pinnate at base, 2–3-pinnate distally. Pinnules dark green, veins hidden; sterile pinnules broader than fertile pinnules, margins flat.

RANGE/HABITAT: NSW (se), Vic, Tas, SA (s), WA (sw). Endemic. Sheltered rock outcrops and rocky slopes in loam.

CAVE FERN *Cheilanthes cavernicola*

Distinctive resprouting fern with broad pale green to almost greyish-green fronds bearing prominent white cottony hairs. Forms spreading, much-branched clumps in secluded/sheltered sites in dissected sandstone. Monsoonal wet-season grower.

ID: Fertile fronds to 40 x 10cm, ±triangular, 3-pinnate at base, 2-pinnate near centre, apex pinnate, thin-textured.

RANGE/HABITAT: NT (n), WA (Kimberley). Endemic. Sheltered rock ledges, rock hollows and shallow caves.

FRAGILE ROCK FERN *Cheilanthes fragillima*

Delicate fern with decorative, lacy, bright green fronds which are brittle and easily damaged. Monsoonal wet-season grower. Plants appear dead in the dry season and regrow rapidly after the first rains of the wet season. AKA *Hemionitis fragillima*.

ID: Fertile fronds to 32 x 14cm, triangular, 3–4-pinnate at base, 2-pinnate/pinnatifid distally, thin-textured, paler underside with conspicuous white hairs.

RANGE/HABITAT: NT (n), WA (Kimberley). Endemic. Sheltered areas in dissected sandstone, crevices, between boulders.

SKELETON FERN *Cheilanthes nitida*

Its delicate appearance belies the hardiness of this fern, which forms small tight clumps, the fronds either crowded in upright groups or more commonly seen dangling from rock crevices. Monsoonal wet-season grower.

ID: Fertile fronds to 36 x 12cm, 2-pinnate at base, rest pinnate with long, widely spreading, narrow dark green pinnae.

RANGE/HABITAT: Qld (n), NT (n). Endemic. Escarpments, sheltered rock faces, rock crevices, moist earthen banks in open forest.

LEATHERY ROCK FERN *Cheilanthes praetermissa*

Highly localised, this resprouting fern grows in small groups in sheltered areas among rocks and boulders. Monsoonal wet season grower. Plants appear dead in the dry season and regrow rapidly after the first rains of the wet season.

ID: Fertile fronds to 30 x 8cm, 2–3-pinnate at base, pinnate/pinnatifid distally, leathery, bright green, paler beneath, veins hidden.

RANGE/HABITAT: NT (n), WA (Kimberley). Endemic. Escarpments, sandstone sheets, crevices, between boulders.

MEMBRANOUS ROCK FERN *Cheilanthes pumilio*

Colonial fern which grows in mixed groups of mature plants and sporelings, each with few (1–5) glabrous arching/pendent fronds. Less tolerant of dryness than other rock ferns and regenerates rapidly from sporelings in favourable conditions. Monsoonal wet-season grower.

ID: Fertile fronds to 15 x 5cm, 1-pinnate throughout or pinnatifid at base, thin-textured/membranous, bright green, paler beneath, veins prominent.

RANGE/HABITAT: Qld (n), NT (n), WA (Kimberley). Endemic. Sheltered rock faces, crevices, wetter forests.

TAPE FERN, BOOTLACE FERN

Haplopteris elongata

Common clumping fern with arching/hanging narrow fronds. Grows on mossy boulders and tree trunks, rotting logs and among the roots of other epiphytes. PKA *Vittaria elongata*.

ID: Rhizomes short- to long-creeping. Fronds simple, to 90 x 1cm, linear, flat in cross-section, green, shiny (occas. dull pale green), tapered to each end, thinly leathery.

RANGE/HABITAT: Qld, NSW (Torres Strait Is. to Casino); NFK, CI, Af, As, Oc. Coast to ranges and tlnds in wetter forests.

RIBBON FERN, SHOESTRING FERN

Haplopteris ensiformis

Similar to the previous sp. but with shorter arching/hanging fronds that widen towards the apex. PKA *Vittaria ensiformis*.

ID: Rhizomes short-creeping. Fronds simple, crowded, suberect to pendulous, to 50 x 0.6cm, linear, often cupped in cross-section, dark green, shiny, tapered to each end, thinly leathery.

RANGE/HABITAT: NT (n), Qld, NSW (Torres Strait Is. to Gosford); Af, As, Oc. Coast to ranges and tlnds in wetter forests.

Small fertile plants.

ROCK SICKLE FERN *Pellaea calidirupium*

Poorly known fern which can be recognised by its glossy, dark green, strongly dimorphic fronds. Short sterile fronds have fewer broader blunt pinnae. Taller fertile fronds have narrower ±triangular pinnae with pointed tips.

ID: Rhizomes long-creeping. Fronds to 50cm long (including stipe), 1-pinnate. Pinnae 15–40 per frond, each to 30 x 12mm.

RANGE/HABITAT: Qld (n to s), NSW, ACT, Vic, Tas; NZ. Terrestrial or lithophytic among rocks in open forest and scrub.

Young plant.

SICKLE FERN *Pellaea falcata*

Widely distributed familiar fern that forms spreading colonies. Often grows in open forest, occas. even in coastal sand dunes but also in denser, wetter forests.

ID: Rhizomes long-creeping. Fronds to 1m long (including stipe), 1-pinnate. Pinnae 30–90 per frond, each to 55 x 12mm, dark green, shiny.

RANGE/HABITAT: Qld (n to Fraser Is.), NSW, ACT, Vic, Tas; LHI. Endemic. Terrestrial or lithophyte in open forest, coastal scrub and rainforest.

LEATHERY SICKLE FERN *Pellaea paradoxa*

A tough fern with leathery fronds that can withstand extended periods of dryness. Often found in rainforest but also in drier more exposed slopes and among rocks. Juvenile plants produce broad, heart-shaped pinnae (often only a single pinna).

ID: Rhizomes long-creeping. Fronds to 65cm long (including stipe), 1-pinnate. Pinnae 7–30 per frond, each to 75 x 25mm, dark green, dull.

RANGE/HABITAT: Qld, NSW (Windsor Tlnd to Sydney); LHI. Endemic.

Sori.

SCALY BUTTON FERN *Pellaea reynoldsii*

Drought-tolerant fern of inland rocky areas. Forms clumps and mats among boulders and in crevices. Decorative bright green fronds are covered with papery scales on both surfaces. Fronds dry and curl in dry times, refreshening quickly after rain. PKA *Paraceterach reynoldsii*. AKA *Hemionitis reynoldsii*.

ID: Rhizomes creeping. Fronds to 25cm long (including stipe), 1-pinnate. Pinnae to 20 x 12mm, blunt. Sori massed along pinna margins.

RANGE/HABITAT: WA, NT, SA. Endemic.

COMB BRAKE *Pteris pacifica*

Decorative clumping fern with erect to spreading dark green fronds. The narrow pinnae, divided nearly to the midrib, resemble the teeth of a comb.

ID: Rhizomes short, erect, with narrow triangular scales. Stipes to 50cm long, green to brownish, grooved. Frond to 1.5m long (including stipe), blades pinnate/pinnatifid, to 40cm across.

RANGE/HABITAT: Qld (Windsor Tlnd to Proserpine); NFK, NG, As, Oc. Coast to ranges and tlnds in rainforest.

BRAID FERN *Pteris platyzomopsis*

Bizarre fern with densely clustered, strongly dimorphic fronds. Short, green, sterile, threadlike fronds are in a basal cluster, whereas tall narrow bluish fertile fronds have small, rounded pinnae, the underside concave with strongly incurved margins. PKA *Platyzoma microphyllum*.

ID: Rhizomes short-creeping, densely covered with golden-brownish hairs. Filiform fronds to 10cm long. Fertile fronds to 60 x 0.6cm.

RANGE/HABITAT: WA (Kimberley), NT (n), Qld, NSW (Weipa to Yetman). Endemic. Open habitats in seasonally inundated, infertile soils.

GIANT BRAKE *Pteris tripartita*

Large fern which grows into a compact clump of tall upright decorative pale green to dark green fronds with a lacy appearance.

ID: Rhizomes short, erect, sturdy. Stipes to 150cm long, green to brownish, grooved. Frond blades 1–2-pinnate/pinnatifid, to 170cm across, broadly triangular. Ultimate segments to 35 x 4mm, margins finely toothed.

RANGE/HABITAT: NT (Kimberley), Qld (Cape Melville to Cardwell, inland to Croydon); CI, Af, As, Oc. Rainforest.

JUNGLE BRAKE *Pteris umbrosa*

Sporadically distributed fern which forms colonies along stream beds and alluvial flats, usually in wetter forests and in rocky areas. Occas. also grows in crevices and on the surface of rocks.

ID: Rhizomes short-creeping, sturdy. Stipes to 80cm long, yellowish brown. Frond blades 1-pinnate to pinnate/pinnatifid, to 120cm long. Pinnae to 35 x 2cm.

RANGE/HABITAT: Qld (ne and se), NSW (ne and se), Vic (e). Endemic. Coast to ranges and tlnds in rainforest.

MORSE FERN *Taenitis pinnata*

Clumping fern which typically grows as a terrestrial in wettish sheltered sites in Qld, but in WA can also be seen as a lithophyte hanging out of clefts and crevices on sandstone cliffs.

ID: Rhizomes short-creeping. Fronds to 80cm long (including long stipes), in two ranks, simple to 1-pinnate. Pinnae 2–7 pairs per frond, each to 20 x 3cm.

RANGE/HABITAT: WA (n), NT (n), Qld (Cape York to Byfield); As, Oc. Streambanks and swampy areas within rainforest.

FERNY AZOLLA *Azolla pinnata*

Free-floating aquatic fern with short feathery roots which extend down into the water. Reproduces freely by fragmentation during warm weather, eventually forming dense floating masses which clog waterways. Frond colour changes seasonally from green to brown or reddish.

ID: Plants triangular in outline. Stems short-creeping, branching freely. Roots with numerous root hairs.

RANGE/HABITAT: NT (n), Qld, NSW, Vic, SA (se), WA (sw); Oc. Still or sluggish water in dams, ponds, lakes, stream margins.

FORKED COMB FERN *Schizaea bifida*

Unusual fern with unbranched or forked, stiffly erect, grass-like fronds topped with distinctive spore-bearing structures (sorophores), each resembling a miniature comb.

ID: Roots fibrous. Rhizomes short-creeping, covered with glossy brown hairs. Fronds clustered, to 55cm long, flattish, winged, green. Fertile heads 5–30mm long, emerging green, ageing to brown.

RANGE/HABITAT: Qld (n to Shelburne Bay), NSW, Vic (s), SA (se), Tas (e); NZ. Infertile sand and peat in open forest, heath and swamps.

ELECTRIC SPIKEMOSS *Selaginella longipinna*

Attractive clumping lycophyte that grows on sheltered banks and in the ground in shady forests. Spreads by wiry rhizomes that support broad, fan-shaped fronds (10–30cm wide). Two layers of small, dark, electric-green leaves cover the stems. Short spike-like strobili occur on the segment tips.

ID: Stems 15–40cm tall. Leaves 2.5–4mm long. Strobili 10–65mm long.

RANGE/HABITAT: Qld (Daintree to Mission Beach). Endemic. Wetter forests, especially rainforest.

SWAMP SPIKEMOSS *Selaginella uliginosa*

Widely distributed common lycophyte that usually grows in moist/wet or swampy places, occas. also drier sites. Produces wiry rhizomes to form spreading patches. Upright branching growths are clothed with tiny, stiff, pointed green leaves which become pinkish-red in bright sun. Short strobili occur on the segment tips.

ID: Stems 5–40cm tall. Leaves 1–3mm long. Strobili 5–25mm long.

RANGE/HABITAT: WA (n), NT (n), Qld (se), NSW, Vic, Tas. Endemic. Heathland, open forest.

Coloured leaves.

FISHBONE JOINTED FERN *Arthropteris beckleri*

Common epiphytic fern that grows in extended strands or spreading patches. Thin, densely hairy/scaly rhizomes support decorative bright green fronds that taper to each end. Starts life as a terrestrial then climbs on trees and rocks.

ID: Rhizomes scandent, c.1mm diam. Fronds to 35 x 3cm, pinnate, shiny, suberect to arching.

RANGE/HABITAT: Qld, NSW (Cape Tribulation to Nowra); As, Oc. Coast to ranges/tlnds in wetter forests.

LESSER JOINTED FERN *Arthropteris palisotii*

Slender fern that starts life in the ground before climbing on rocks and trees. Juvenile fronds are much shorter and have fewer pinnae than mature fronds.

ID: Rhizomes scandent, c.1mm diam. densely scaly. Fronds to 30 x 10cm, pinnate, arching/pendent, thinly leathery. Pinnae blunt. Apical segment enlarged.

RANGE/HABITAT: Qld, NSW (Iron Ra to Illawarra region); CI, Af, As, Oc. Sporadic. Coast to ranges/tlnds in wetter forests.

Juvenile fronds.

JOINTED FERN *Arthropteris tenella*

Coarse fern that climbs on mossy rocks and trees forming extended strands. Its thickish rhizome covered with red-brown scales supports broad dark green shiny fronds with widely spreading pinnae.

ID: Rhizomes scandent, to 4mm diam. densely scaly. Fronds to 50 x 20cm, pinnate, leathery. Pinnae pointed.

RANGE/HABITAT: Qld, NSW (Windsor Tlnd to Kiama); LHI., NFK, NZ. Coast to ranges/tlnds in wetter forests.

Climbing.

MUELLER'S TECTARIA *Tectaria confluens*

Clumping fern with decorative, dark green, shiny fronds that are more or less triangular and ornately lobed. Often grows in patches among rocks and on sheltered earthen banks with the fronds spilling down the slope. PKA *Tectaria muelleri*.

ID: Rhizomes short, erect. Stipe to 45cm long. Frond laminae to 45 x 40cm, triangular, pinnately lobed, thinly leathery. Apical part multilobed.

RANGE/HABITAT: Qld (Iron Ra. to Mackay). Endemic. Coast to ranges/ tlnds in rainforest.

Sori.

SKIRRET FERN *Tectaria siifolia*

Uncommon fern with a very restricted distribution in Aust. Recognised by its strongly dimorphic shiny dark green fronds. Fertile fronds are smaller and held above the sterile fronds on longer stipes, the underside with numerous large brown sori.

ID: Rhizomes short-creeping. Fronds to 50 x 30cm. Sterile fronds larger and more deeply lobed than fertile fronds and on shorter stipes.

RANGE/HABITAT: NT (Arafura Swamp), Qld (Iron Ra.); CI, As, Oc. Dense lowland rainforest.

CARDBOARD FERN *Abacopteris aspera*

Decorative fern readily recognised by its knobbly rootstock and erect/arching, stiff, papery, dull green fronds. Large spreading pinnae have a rounded base, conspicuous raised veins and shortly pointed apex. PKA *Pronephrium asperum*.

ID: Rhizomes creeping, thick, woody. Fronds pinnate, to 200 x 70cm, dull green, somewhat leathery. Pinnae 6–10 pairs, to 35 x 6cm, margins smooth to bluntly toothed.

RANGE/HABITAT: Qld (Bloomfield to Cardwell); As, Oc. Rainforest.

ROVE FERN *Amblovenatum terminans*

Coarse fern that forms small spreading clumps in wet areas along stream banks and in open patches in rainforest. PKA *Amphineuron terminans*.

ID: Rhizomes long-creeping. Fronds pinnate, erect/arching, to 150 x 40cm, bright green to dark green, ending in a pinna-like growth. Pinnae to 20 x 2cm, deeply lobed, sori grouped near apex.

RANGE/HABITAT: Qld (Torres Strait Is. to Cardwell); As, Oc. Rainforest.

FECUND FERN *Ampelopteris prolifera*

Unusual fern that forms spreading patches and thickets in wet sites. Extends by the production of sprawling fronds many metres long and proliferates by numerous buds and plantlets that develop along their length.

ID: Rhizomes short-creeping. Fronds pinnate, pale green, of two forms; long fronds (no terminal leaflet) and short fronds with a terminal leaflet.

RANGE/HABITAT: WA (nw), NT (n), Qld (Daintree to Brisbane), ?NSW; As, Oc. Streambanks and swamps in open forest.

CHINGIA FERN *Chingia australis*

Spectacular but rare fern with pale green to dark green, broad lacy fronds. Can grow as scattered individuals but occas. forms impressive stands beside small streams.

ID: Trunk to 30 x 8cm. Fronds pinnate, erect/arching, 1–2.5m long, 50–60cm wide. Pinnae to 33 x 3cm, margins lobed for about ⅓ distance to midrib, apex drawn into a long point.

RANGE/HABITAT: Qld (Daintree to Russell R.). Endemic. Open patches in lowland rainforest.

BINUNG FERN *Christella dentata*

Widely distributed, common fern that grows individually or forms localised spreading groups. Often in semi-sheltered situations but also on exposed slopes and banks. The basal 2–4 pairs of pinnae reduce progressively in size. Naturalises readily.

ID: Rhizomes short-creeping. Fronds pinnatifid, arching, to 100 x 30cm, dark green, thin textured. Pinnae to 10 x 1.8cm.

RANGE/HABITAT: WA, NT, Qld (n to Iron Ra.), NSW, Vic, SA (se); LHI, NFK, Af, As, Oc. Open forest, streambanks, inland gorges, rainforest margins.

SPICE FERN *Christella parasitica*

Interesting fern with bright green shiny fronds that are sticky when young and with a spicy odour when crushed. Forms clumps in wetter areas but also on sheltered earthen banks and near streams, occas. in pasture.

ID: Rhizomes creeping. Fronds pinnatifid, arching, to 80 x 30cm, green, somewhat leathery. Pinnae to 16 x 2cm, lobed.

RANGE/HABITAT: Qld (Cooktown to Gold Coast); LHI, NFK, As, Oc. Streambanks, swamps, rainforest margins.

SWAMP SHIELD FERN *Cyclosorus interruptus*

Common harsh fern that forms large, spreading patches in seepage sites, wet caves, springs and swamps, often in exposed sunny situations.

ID: Rhizomes slender, long-creeping, much branched. Fronds pinnatifid, erect/arching, to 120 x 30cm, green to brownish green, somewhat leathery. Pinnae to 15 x 1.8cm, lobed.

RANGE/HABITAT: Qld (n to Cooktown), NSW (ne), Vic (sw), NT (mainly n, also Central Aust.), WA (mainly nw); pantropical. Permanently wet sites.

LIME FERN *Pneumatopteris pennigera*

Rare fern with a trunk that can reach 1m tall and pale green, arching/spreading fronds, each with a dark central rachis and spreading lobed pinnae. Grows in isolated populations, usually among limestone or in calcareous soil.

ID: Rhizomes erect, trunk-like. Fronds 1-pinnate, to 110 x 15cm (including stipe). Pinnae to 9 x 2cm.

RANGE/HABITAT: Qld (se), ?NSW (unknown), Vic (sw), Tas (nw, King Is.); NZ. Soaks, moist flats and streambanks in forests.

Sori.

GLOSSARY

Acuminate: With a long, drawn-out point.

Acute: With a short, sharp point.

Arborescent: Tree-like.

Articulate: Jointed.

Auriculate: Bearing auricles or ear-like appendages.

Axillary: Borne in an axil.

Bipinnate: Twice pinnately divided.

Bulbil: Small bulb-like growth borne on a frond and developing into a plantlet.

Calcareous: An excess of lime in a soil.

Circinnate: Coiled, as in young fern fronds.

Clathrate: Lattice-like.

Colonial: Colony-forming.

Compound leaf: A leaf with two or more separate divisions or separate leaflets.

Coriaceus: Leathery in texture.

Costa: Midvein of a pinna.

Costule: Midvein of a pinnule or lesser segment.

Crozier: Coiled young frond.

Dentate: Toothed.

Dichotomous: Regularly forking into equal branches.

Dimorphic: Producing two forms.

Elongate: Drawn out in length.

Endemic: Confined to a given region.

Entire: Simple and undivided.

Epiphyte: A plant growing on or attached to other plants, but not parasitic.

Exindusiate: Without an indusium.

False indusium: Covering over sori formed by a reflexed leaf margin.

Fertile: Bearing spores.

Frond: A fern leaf, including the supporting stalk (stipe).

Genus: A taxonomic group of closely related species.

Glabrous: Without hairs, smooth.

Glaucous: Bluish to bluish-grey.

Indusium: The membranous covering of a sorus.

Lamina: The expanded part of a leaf.

Leaflet: Segment of a compound leaf.

Lithophyte: Plant growing on rocks or cliffs.

Lobe: A rounded or blunt segment.

Lobed: Divided into lobes.

Lycophyte: Plants related to ferns but with small leaves instead of true fronds and with spores borne on specialised sporophylls (families Isoetaceae, Lycopodiaceae, Psilotaceae and Selaginellaceae).

Marginal: Attached to or near the edge.

Membranous: Thin.

Nest fronds: Sterile fronds which trap litter.

Palmate: Divided or lobed like a hand.

Peltate: Shield-like, attached by a central stalk.

Pendent: Hanging downwards.

Phyllopodium: An outgrowth which joins a stipe to a rhizome.

Pinna: A primary segment of a divided leaf.

Pinnate: Once divided with the divisions extending to the central stem (rachis).

Pinnatifid: Once divided, but with the divisions not extending to the central stem (rachis).

Pinnule: A secondary or higher pinna, an ultimate segment.

Proliferous: Producing buds or new plants vegetatively.

Rachis: The main axis of the lamina of a simple or compound leaf.

Resprouter: Plants that die back to storage root system to avoid hot, dry conditions, regrowing when conditions are favourable.

Rhizome: An underground stem.

Scale: A dry flattened papery structure borne on various parts of a fern.

Scandent: Climbing.

Sessile: Without a stalk.

Simple: Undivided, in one piece, as in leaves.

Soral flap Specialised fertile lobe subtending the sori in *Adiantum*.

Sorophore: Sorus bearing structure in *Schizaea*.

Sorus: A cluster or grouping of sporangia.

Species: A group of closely related plants with a common set of features that sets them apart from another species.

Sporangium/ia: A case in which spores are formed.

Sporophore: Sporangia-bearing structure in Ophioglossaceae.

Spore: Tiny reproductive structure that lacks an embryo.

Sporeling: A young fern.

Sporophyll: A specialised leaf that bears spores or a spore-bearing structure.

Stipe: The leaf stalk from the rhizome to the base of the lamina.
Stipule: Bract(s) at the base of a stipe.
Strobilus: Cone-shaped spore-bearing structure.
Sucker: A shoot arising from the roots below ground level.
Synganium/a: Fruiting structure formed by the fusion of sporangia (*Psilotum*, *Tmesipteris*, *Marattia*).
Terrestrial: Growing in the ground.

FURTHER READING

Andrews, S.B. (1990). *Ferns of Queensland*, Queensland Department of Primary Industries, Brisbane, Australia.

Field, R.A. (2020). Classification and typification of Australian lycophytes and ferns based on Pteridophyte Phylogeny Group Classification PPG 1, *Aust. Syst. Bot.* 33: 1–102.

Garrett, M. (1996). *The Ferns of Tasmania, their ecology and distribution*, Tasmanian Forest Research Council, Inc., Tasmania, Australia.

Jones, D.L. (1987). *Encyclopaedia of Ferns*, Lothian Publishing Coy, Melbourne, Australia.

Jones, D.L., and Clemesha, S.C. (1982). *Australian Ferns and Fern Allies*, A.H. and A.W. Reed Pty Ltd, Sydney, Australia.

McCarthy, P.M. (Ed.) (1998). Ferns, Gymnosperms and Allied Groups, *Flora of Australia*, vol. 48, ABRS and CSIRO, Melbourne, Australia.

INDEX

N

O

P

Q

OTHER TITLES IN THE SERIES

Animals of Australia
Ken Stepnell
ISBN 978 1 92151 754 9

Beetles of Australia
Paul Zborowski
ISBN 978 1 76079 611 2

Birds of Australia
Ken Stepnell
ISBN 978 1 92151 753 2

Butterflies of Australia
Paul Zborowski
ISBN 978 1 92554 694 1

Frogs of Australia
Marion Anstis
ISBN 978 1 92151 790 7

Insects of Australia
Paul Zborowski
ISBN 978 1 92554 644 6

Lilies of Australia
David L Jones
ISBN 978 1 76079 617 4

Lizards of Australia
Steve K Wilson
ISBN 978 1 92554 657 6

Sea Fishes of Australia
Nigel Marsh
ISBN 978 1 76079 631 0

Snakes of Australia
Gerry Swan
ISBN 978 1 92151 789 1

Spiders of Australia
Volker W Framenau and Melissa L Thomas
ISBN 978 1 92554 603 3

Trees of Australia
David L Jones
ISBN 978 1 92554 688 0

Wild Flowers of Australia
Ken Stepnell
ISBN 978 1 92151 755 6

For details of these books and hundreds of other Natural History titles see **newhollandpublishers.com**